A COMPLAINT FREE WORLD

A COMPLAINT FREE WORLD

HOW TO STOP COMPLAINING
AND START ENJOYING
THE LIFE YOU ALWAYS WANTED

WILL BOWEN

THREE RIVERS PRESS

NEW YORK

Published in the United States by Three Rivers Press,
an imprint of the Crown Publishing Group,
a division of Random House, Inc., New York.

www.threeriverspress.com
www.crownpublishing.com

THREE RIVERS PRESS and the Tugboat design
are registered trademarks of Random House, Inc.

"Complaint Free," "A Complaint Free World," and "Complaint Free
bracelets" are trademarks of Lamplighter, Inc. All rights reserved.

Originally published in hardcover in different form
in the United States by Doubleday Books,
a division of Random House, Inc., New York, in 2007.

Cartoon on page viii copyright © 2007 The Kansas City Star

Photo of Maya Angelou on page xiv copyright © John Gladman

Cartoon on page 126 © Jean Browman

Library of Congress Cataloging-in-Publication Data
Bowen, Will.
  A complaint free world : how to stop complaining and start enjoying
the life you always wanted / Will Bowen. — 1st pbk. ed.
    p. cm.
1. Criticism, Personal. 2. Faultfinding. 3. Self-help techniques. 4. Life
skills. 5. Performance—Psychological aspects. I. Title.
  BF637.C74B69 2012
  158.1—dc23
                              2012020653

ISBN 978-0-7704-3639-1
eISBN 978-0-7704-3646-9

Printed in the United States of America

Book design by Jaclyn Reyes
Cover photograph: Tom Grill/Tetra Images/Corbis

20   19   18   17   16   15   14   13

First Paperback Edition

For my daughter Lia,
her children yet to be,
and their children;
each of whom will live
in a subsequently happier,
more Complaint Free World.

CONTENTS

"PURPLE ?!"

PREFACE

A Complaint Free World's vision is to share Complaint Free bracelets with sixty million people—1 percent of the world's population. If we can positively transform the attitudes of just 1 percent of our world's people, it will have a ripple effect, raising the consciousness of everyone.

As of this writing we are over ten million bracelets.

The power of calling something into reality by focusing single-mindedly on it was demonstrated in my own life as we approached the six-millionth-bracelet milestone. The Board of Directors for A Complaint Free World wanted to present the six millionth bracelet to someone who inspired us, someone whose words and example typified Complaint Free living. After a brief discussion, the choice was obvious and unanimous—Dr. Maya Angelou, former United States Poet Laureate and mentor to Oprah Winfrey.

When we first began A Complaint Free World, we adopted Dr. Angelou's quote "If you don't like something change it. If you can't change it, change your attitude. Don't complain" as our motto.

> "Complaining lets a bully know that a victim is in the neighborhood."
>
> —MAYA ANGELOU

The challenge was that none of us knew Dr. Angelou. We began to do some research and found that many authors and nonprofits had attempted to connect with her with no luck. Speaking to publishers and agents got us nowhere.

At this point we could have given up or at least begun to consider other options. But we refused to be dissuaded. Rather, I began to tell people I was going to personally present the six millionth Complaint Free bracelet to Dr. Maya Angelou. Many asked, "How do you know her?" To which I responded, honestly, "I don't."

"Then how are you going to meet with her to give her the bracelet?"

Again, I spoke the truth, "I have no idea. But it's *going* to happen."

Whenever I had a free moment, I imagined meeting Dr. Angelou. I had seen her on television when she read her poem

"On the Pulse of Morning" at President Clinton's 1993 inauguration. I knew she was a mentor to Oprah Winfrey. I knew she was a famous author and educator, but I did not know her, nor did I know anyone who knew her. Nonetheless, whenever people asked how A Complaint Free World was progressing, I enthusiastically told them that we were approaching 10 percent of our sixty-million-bracelet goal and that I was going to present the six millionth bracelet to Maya Angelou.

At a conference, I bumped into an old friend and told her my intention. She did not inquire as to how I knew Dr. Angelou. She did not ask how I intended to make this happen. Rather, she smiled as she started to walk away and said simply, "Tell her I said hello."

I snapped my head around and nearly shouted, "You know Dr. Angelou?"

"I used to book her when she came into town to speak. I've stayed in touch with her niece," she said.

I then poured out my story of trying to reach Dr. Angelou and how we had hit walls with every attempt.

"I can't promise anything," she said, "but I'll see what I can do."

As you'll see, not only did I meet Dr. Angelou, but I enjoyed a pleasant afternoon speaking with her in her home in Winston-Salem, North Carolina.

How did this happen?

Who cares!

We simply made a decision that seemed far beyond our capacity to realize, and yet because we would not let the idea go, because we saw this as a done deal—a fait accompli—it came to pass.

I not only held the vision of meeting Dr. Angelou and getting to honor her with the six millionth bracelet, I put this energy out into the world by telling other people that this was—not might, *was*—going to happen.

When I met Dr. Angelou at her home in Winston-Salem, we discussed the vision of A Complaint Free World. I told her that the bracelet we presented her symbolized our being, at that time, 10 percent of the way to our goal and then asked how she thought the world might be different when we reach our goal of sixty million. She said,

How do I think the world would be, if 1 percent of the world's population was Complaint Free?

Einstein said, "No genius has ever used more than 18 percent of the brain." But today's scientists say no genius has ever used more than 10 percent of the brain. The majority of us mumble and get along with 5, 6, or 7 percent.

If we've been able to stay alive at all, alive and future thinking, alive and having enough courage to care for each other, enough courage to love, imagine who we would be if 1 percent of six billion people were Complaint Free.

What would happen?

I tell you one thing, I think war would be laughed out of the room. I think the very word . . . "war."

If someone said, '"War? You mean I'm supposed to kill somebody simply because he doesn't agree with me? Hah! I don't think so!"

Just imagine, people would speak more kindly to each other. Courtesy would be invited back into the living room, and to the bedroom and to the children's room and into the kitchen.

If 1 percent of our world was Complaint Free, we would care more about the children and realize that every child is our child; the black one and the white one, the pretty one and the plain one, the Asian and Muslim, the Japanese and the Jewish—everyone is our child.

If we were just 1 percent Complaint Free, we would stop blaming others for our mistakes and hating them because, in our minds, they caused the mistake.

Just imagine if we laughed more frequently, if we had the unmitigated courage to touch each other, it would be just the beginning of paradise—now.

Presenting Dr. Maya Angelou with the six millionth Complaint Free bracelet

INTRODUCTION

If you don't like something change it.
If you can't change it, change your attitude. Don't complain.

—MAYA ANGELOU

I n your hands you hold the secret to transforming your life.
It's been nearly five years since I first typed those words, and I am more convinced of their truth today than ever. Over the past half decade, more than ten million people in 106 countries have embraced the Complaint Free concept and, as a result, transformed their families, their jobs, their churches, their schools, and, most significantly, their own lives.

They have used the simple idea of putting a purple silicone bracelet on their wrist and then switching it from wrist to wrist every time they complained, until they completed twenty-one consecutive days without complaining, criticizing, or gossiping. In so doing, they have formed a new habit. By becoming conscious of and changing their words, they have

> **VOICES**
>
> *I'm a sophomore at Omaha Northwest High School, in Nebraska. Yesterday we had a gunshot go off at our school, and a few students and I would like to try your 21 days of no complaining. I was wondering if I could get 5 bracelets.*
>
> —NAME WITHHELD

changed their thoughts and begun to create their lives by design.

In 2006, while minister of Christ Church Unity in Kansas City, Missouri, I was doing a series on prosperity based on Edwene Gaines's powerful book *The Four Spiritual Laws of Prosperity*. In her book she makes the point that most people claim to want prosperity, but spend most of their waking hours complaining about what they already have. In so doing, they repel rather than attract prosperity.

> "If you're not happy with what you have, then why would you want more?"
>
> —DR. WAYNE DYER

Complaining never attracts what you want; it perpetuates what you do not want. As Wayne Dyer put it, "If you're not happy with what you have, then why would you want more?" The first step toward prosperity in all its forms is to be grateful for what we currently possess, and we can't complain about what we have and be grateful at the same time.

Since the first edition of this book was published, a lot has transpired. More than ten million Complaint Free bracelets have been distributed to people in 106 countries.

We have been featured on *Oprah*, ABC *World News Tonight*, NBC's *Today* show (twice), CBS's *Sunday Morning*, the Fox News Channel, the Dr. Oz radio show, National Public Radio, and in hundreds of newspaper, radio, and television stories. In fact, for several years I was interviewed, on average, three times each and every week by media around the world.

Stories about living Complaint Free have appeared in *Newsweek*, *Chicken Soup for the Soul*, the *Wall Street Journal*, *People*, *O*, *Self*, *Good Housekeeping*, and other books and periodicals too numerous to count.

Steven Colbert took shots at us on *The Colbert Report*. Dennis Miller made a joke about not liking the color of our bracelets—a typical Miller tongue-in-cheek jab making a complaint about no complaint bracelets. On *60 Minutes*, Andy Rooney quipped, "If this guy [me] has his way, I'll be out of a job."

Oprah Winfrey challenged her makeup artist to use one of our bracelets to try and go twenty-one consecutive days without complaining. And Oprah's *O* magazine's South Africa edition distributed fifty thousand of our bracelets to its readership.

Twice, Congress has entertained a bill to make the day before Thanksgiving Complaint Free Wednesday in the United States. And, although the national proclamation has yet to pass (we are certain it will), dozens of cities small and large have designated Complaint Free Wednesday as a way to transition from one day without complaining into our national day of gratitude.

We created a free school curriculum, which has been downloaded and used by teachers at thousands of schools around the world to transform their students and their schools. Businesses who have adopted the Complaint Free philosophy have seen improved morale and increased profits even in the worst economy since the Great Depression. For them, we now have a *Complaint Free Organizations* program, which is also downloadable free from our website. It has been utilized by businesses small and large, civic groups, and every type of group or organization you can imagine.

> "Nobility comes not from being superior to another; true nobility comes from being superior to one's former self."
>
> —HINDU SAYING

Churches of every faith have conducted series and classes on Complaint Free living. I was recently in another city and had dinner at an Indian restaurant where all of the employees were wearing our bracelets. When I asked our waiter where he got his bracelet, he responded, "Our Hindu temple gave them out." For them, we created a *Complaint Free Churches* program; also a free download at our website.

For the last several years, I have delivered, on average, ten to fifteen speeches per year to audiences of up to four thousand people. I have been fortunate to share the Complaint Free concept as a keynote address at conventions, rallies, and staff development programs to Fortune 20 companies, software firms, direct marketing companies, automobile manufacturers, major accounting firms, statewide school psychologist associations, government agencies, utility companies, hospitals, banks, and many, many more.

I have traveled to China three times in the last twelve months speaking to vast audiences there about the damaging effects of complaining, why we complain, and how to become Complaint Free. The first edition of this book was the biggest selling book in China in 2009 and the second biggest selling book there in 2010.

We have created a computer widget that is free for download at our website. The widget does not harvest any information about you or your computer and it doesn't plant any spyware. It simply resides on your desktop, giving you a visual reminder of what day you are on along your twenty-one-day Complaint Free journey. And, as a bonus, every day I write a short message that pops up on the widget to help you stay focused and inspired.

In the early days, when the Complaint Free idea first

began to evolve from a spark into a flame, volunteers stepped forward to pack the bracelets. Dozens of people donated their every Saturday to send the bracelets out. In the summer, people who heard about A Complaint Free World flew to Kansas City to spend their vacations packing bracelets. Tens of thousands of bracelets were sent out each week, and every week the number of requests grew.

At first, the enthusiasm people had for the Complaint Free concept stunned and elated everyone. Then it became obvious that this was not going to fade, but rather it would continue to grow. At that point we thanked our volunteers, who released a sigh of relief, and moved the packing of the bracelets to a sheltered workshop. Later, we hired an employee to handle the requests.

She is our only employee. The rest of the work is still handled by volunteers.

Incidentally, if you were familiar with the Complaint Free movement from our early days, you probably have noticed that about three years ago we shifted from giving the bracelets away and asking for a donation, to where we now charge for them. The reason for this was that so many people were requesting the bracelets (a whopping two million in just twenty-four hours after we appeared on *Oprah*) that we did not have the money to purchase and send them. Since about 98 percent of people who made donations did so only *after* receiving their bracelets, and since we did not have the money up front to first buy and ship the bracelets (shipping is our greatest expense), we had to switch to selling them.

We found that most people ordered about ten bracelets, so we switched to selling ten bracelets for ten dollars. As a 501(c)(3) nonprofit, we still accept donations (none of the money goes to me), and we are grateful that the donations continue to come in.

One of the most common questions I am asked is "Did you see this becoming this big when you began?"

The answer is "No."

I was recently interviewed by a highly respected periodical that inspires authors to improve their writing, acquire a literary agent, and get their books published. The interviewer asked, "So, can you tell our readers how they, too, can create a worldwide movement?" I burst into uncontrollable laughter.

When I had composed myself, I responded, "No, I have no idea."

True, when we handed out the first 250 bracelets on July 23, 2006, I said, "We will become a ripple of no-complaining which will spread around the world," but people make such grandiose statements all the time. My ego would like to think it was purely the power of my intention that caused this, but there is much more to the story.

How did a simple idea begun in Kansas City, Missouri, of

all places send a shock wave throughout every corner of the world, and why, six years later, does it continue?

Why in just a few short months did our Facebook followers shoot from zero to, as of this writing, nearly twenty-five thousand and continue to grow daily?

Why do Google alerts still pour in stating that people are forming groups and book clubs to support one another in becoming Complaint Free?

Why, half a decade after its inception, do dozens of people discover and Tweet about this idea ten to twenty times a day, often in languages I don't even recognize?

I have given this question a lot of thought and believe I have an answer. The answer to this question is the core concept of this book and the Complaint Free movement. There are two reasons for the continued global impact of this idea:

1. There is too much complaining in the world.
2. The world is not the way we would like it to be.

I believe the two are correlated. We are so busy focusing on what is wrong in the world, as evidenced by our complaints, that we are perpetuating these problems.

We are obsessed with what is wrong. We complain about anything and everything, and as a result we keep focusing on our problems. Contrary to popular belief, complaining does not lead to solving our problems. Rather it concretizes our challenges and justifies our inaction in doing anything to make things better.

Currently, the world is obsessed with negativity. It is like a cloud that shrouds the sky, preventing us from seeing the light that would illuminate and resolve our challenges.

Before you read any further, I should offer you a warning. By reading this book, you are going to become more aware of negativity and complaining. In fact, it will be as if someone turned up the volume on complaining in your world. However, once you are aware of it, you can choose whether or not to participate.

When I was a boy, nearly everyone smoked cigarettes. I can remember going to the pediatrician to have my asthma checked. Ole Doc Castles would place a stethoscope on my chest and wheeze, "Breathe deeply." He wheezed because my doctor would typically have a cigarette dangling from his lips.

Most people, including doctors treating young boys for asthma, smoked back then. Everyone and everything; people's clothes, their hair, breath, homes, furniture, cars, offices, movie theaters, and more smelled of cigarette smoke, and yet we were so used it that we barely noticed. Today, hardly any public place in the United States permits smoking. If you go to a country where people still smoke freely, it's astounding how pungent and noxious the smell of smoke permeating everything can be. And yet the people in those countries, just like people in the United States decades ago, aren't aware of the cloying smell of cigarette smoke.

As you move through your Complaint Free journey, you are going begin to notice how negative most people's attitudes and comments are—including your own! The negativity is already there, you will just become aware of it for perhaps the first time. Right now complaining is like cigarette odor. It surrounds you at all times, but now you are going to begin to notice it.

You will really become aware of our penchant for negativity when you watch what passes for "the news."

A couple of years ago, I was invited to speak to the residents of an economically challenged city in Canada. The day of my speech, I had lunch with the mayor and other dignitaries from the city, including the publisher of the local newspaper. After lots of discussion about the importance of thinking and speaking positively, the newspaper publisher leaned over and whispered sheepishly to me, "Will, I hate to admit it but if we run a headline that says CRISIS! it will outsell one that reads GREAT NEWS! ten-to-one."

> "The tendency to whining and complaining may be taken as the surest sign symptom of little souls and inferior intellects."
>
> —LORD JEFFREY

I told the publisher not to feel guilty. He wasn't telling people which papers to buy. He and other members of the media have just found a way to tap in to people's negative bias. Our appetite is for what is wrong and what is bad, and we seek to be reminded of these things for some very good reasons, which I will explain in this book.

I know a man who watches CNN twenty-four hours a day—literally. He even sleeps with it roaring from the television at the foot of his bed. He is one of the most fearful and negative people I know.

For myself, I opted several years ago not to watch, read, or listen to what others call "the news." What we receive is *not* news. Bestselling author Esther Hicks recently commented that if the news were an accurate reflection of the day's events, twenty-nine minutes and fifty-nine seconds of a thirty-minute broadcast would be good things that occurred, and the bad news would be just a one-second blip on the screen. What we call news is actually Bad News. To get the most from your Complaint Free journey, I encourage you stop watching, listening to, and/or reading the Bad News.

Don't worry, if something significant happens, someone will tell you. I was in Mwanza, Tanzania, the day that Michael Jackson died. I went to donate blood early that morning and the manager of the facility ran out to tell me of Jackson's death. I was on the other side of the world, and someone made sure I knew what had happened, so if something important occurs, especially something negative, other people will ache to tell you about it.

You've got to begin to treat your mind like a garden. In *As a Man Thinketh*, James Allen put it brilliantly:

A man's mind may be likened to a garden, which may be intelligently cultivated or allowed to run wild; but whether cultivated or neglected, it must, and will, bring forth. If no useful seeds are put into it, then an abundance of useless weed seeds will fall therein, and will continue to produce their kind.

Negative thoughts are seeds we plant in the world through complaining. They will produce. Therefore, guard your thoughts. Protect them. Shield them from the negativity of others and what some call "news." And begin now to shift your comments from what is destructive to what is constructive.

> Negative thoughts are seeds we plant in the world through complaining. They will produce.

Your thoughts create your life and your words indicate what you are thinking.

The world is awakening to a new way of being and a new level of existence, and the first step toward this transformation is to stop giving energy to what is wrong by talking incessantly about it.

Our thoughts create our lives, and our words indicate what we are thinking. If you get nothing else from this book, this idea alone will transform your life.

In every moment, you are creating your life with the thoughts you give primary *attention* to.

You have probably heard of the blockbuster movie and/or book *The Secret* by Rhonda Byrne. The so-called secret is that we move in the direction of our thoughts, and the universe responds by manifesting what we think about.

The Secret struck a chord with the world. To me, it is actually a modern retelling of Earl Nightingale's 1956 recording, *The Strangest Secret*. Nightingale said that his inspiration for *The Strangest Secret* came from *Think and Grow Rich* by Napoleon Hill. Hill gave credit to Andrew Carnegie, Henry Ford, and others. So this idea is anything but new. It seems to be reaching a critical mass in our universal understanding today, but thousands of great philosophers and teachers have told us this "secret" for millennia:

"As thou hast believed, so be it done unto thee."

—JESUS, MATTHEW 8:13

"The universe is change; our life is what our thoughts make it."

—MARCUS AURELIUS

"We are shaped by our thoughts; we become what we think."

—THE BUDDHA

"Change your thoughts and you change your world."

—NORMAN VINCENT PEALE

"You are today where your thoughts have brought you; you will be tomorrow where your thoughts take you."

—JAMES ALLEN

"We become what we think about."

—EARL NIGHTINGALE

"The highest possible stage in moral culture is when we recognize that we ought to control our thoughts."

—CHARLES DARWIN

"Why are we Masters of our fate, the captains of our souls? Because we have the power to control our thoughts."

—ALFRED A. MONTAPERT

What you articulate, you demonstrate. Our thoughts create our lives, and our words indicate what we are thinking. If you will change your words, your thoughts will follow and you will change your life.

People fall along a great continuum of being positive or negative. Having spoken to tens of thousands of people around the world, I have not had one person yet come up and say to me, "I'm the most negative person you will ever meet." It seems people have a blind spot as to when they are being pessimistic rather than optimistic.

> What you articulate, you demonstrate.

Their words may reveal this to others, but they don't hear it. They may gripe constantly—prior to my completing the twenty-one-day challenge, I was one of them—but most people, myself included, think they are positive, upbeat, optimistic, and sanguine.

It is vital that we control our minds in order to consciously create our lives. The Complaint Free bracelet is not a symbol you sport on your wrist to inform others that you support living Complaint Free. Rather, properly used, it is a tool that will make you aware of when and how often you complain, so you can stop.

When you go through the practice of moving your bracelet from wrist to wrist, over and over, time after time, you will begin to notice your words. In so doing, you will become aware of your thoughts. Your purple bracelet sets a trap for your negativity so it can be caught and, in time, released, never to return.

It is doubtful you can name a life situation that has not

been improved by people who have stayed with the process of becoming Complaint Free. Better health, more satisfying relationships, career advancement, feeling more serene and joyous . . . Sound good? It's not only possible; it's probable. Consciously striving to reformat your mental hard drive is not easy, but start now and in a short period of time—time that will pass anyway—you can have the life you've always dreamed of having.

"A jug fills drop by drop."

—BUDDHIST SAYING

Go to our website at www.AComplaintFreeWorld.org to order your Complaint Free bracelets. Here's how to use the bracelet as a tool for your growth and transformation:

1. Begin to wear the bracelet on either wrist. You are now on Day 1 of your journey to twenty-one consecutive days.
2. When (not if) you catch yourself complaining, criticizing, gossiping, or being sarcastic, move the bracelet to the other wrist and start again. You are back on Day 1.
3. Stay with it. It typically takes four to eight months to reach twenty-one consecutive days.

Why twenty-one days?

Scientists believe that it takes approximately twenty-one days of a consistent behavior for it to become habitual. Ironically, this is how long it takes for a chicken egg to hatch.

Don't be discouraged. If you are honest with yourself, you will discover that it may take you days, weeks, even months to get to Day 2. Then you'll complain and be back on Day 1. But it won't take you nearly as long this time to get to Day 2, and your success will begin to compound on itself, making it easier for you to stay with it.

Most people's Complaint Free patterns look like this: Day 1 . . . Day 1 . . . Day 1 . . . 1 . . . 1 . . . 1 . . . 1 . . . 1 . . . 1 . . . 1 . . . 1 . . . 1 . . . 1 . . . 1 . . . **Day 2!** Back to Day 1 . . . Day 1 . . . Day 1 . . . 1 . . . Day 2 . . . Day 3 . . . Day 4 . . . Day 1 . . . Day 2 . . . Day 3 . . . Day 4 . . . Day 5 . . . Day 1, etc.

Waiting for life to improve before undertaking the twenty-one-day Complaint Free challenge is like waiting until you are in great shape to begin a regimen of diet and exercise.

Some people have told me that they are going to wait until life gets better and then work at becoming Complaint Free. This is ludicrous. Waiting for life to improve before undertaking the twenty-one-day Complaint Free challenge is like waiting until you are in great shape to begin a regimen of diet and exercise.

You want your life to improve? The surest and best tool is a Complaint Free bracelet. Order one at www.AComplaintFree World.org. But don't wait until it arrives. Put a rubber band on your wrist or a coin in your pocket. With every complaint, move the rubber band to the other wrist or switch the coin to another pocket.

Here are some keys to success:

1. **Switch your bracelet with every *spoken* complaint.** Some people try to make this more difficult than it should be by switching their bracelet with every negative thought. Over time, your negative thoughts will lessen significantly, but move the bracelet only when you complain, criticize, gossip, or say something sarcastic *aloud*.

2. **Always know what day you are on.** People who are serious about becoming Complaint Free always know "I'm on Day 1," or "I'm on Day 12." People who fail say things like "I think I'm on Day 8, but I'm not sure." If you don't know what day you're on, you're not following this seriously. If you need help monitoring your progress, download our free computer widget. It will keep you on track, and as I mentioned, you'll get a daily shot of inspiration from me. Oh, and when you reach twenty-one consecutive days without complaining, the widget erupts into animated fireworks to celebrate your achievement.

3. **Don't be a bracelet cop.** This is not about what other people are or are not doing. If you want to point out another

person's complaint and tell that person to switch his or her bracelet, switch your bracelet first!

4. **Don't be clever.** I've known people who try and circumvent the system by wearing a bracelet on both wrists so they don't have to switch. Or when they catch themselves complaining, they quickly complain again so as not to have to move the bracelet. I've even heard of people who when they catch themselves complaining, say they will start again tomorrow and declare the rest of the day a "free day." These little ploys (funny though some of them may be) diminish rather than increase your likelihood of succeeding.

Switch your bracelet with *every* complaint. The average person complains fifteen to thirty times a day, so get used to switching that bracelet. Think of a soldier marching: Left! Right! Left wrist! Right wrist! And so on. When I first took the twenty-one-day challenge, I switched my bracelet so often it looked like I had some sort of nervous condition. I moved mine so much that my bracelet wore out. In fact, I was doing a television interview, and when the producer asked me to demonstrate the process of moving the bracelet from one wrist to the other, my bracelet, which was frayed from switching, popped—*fwang!*—and shot over the cameraman's head.

It's the act of moving the bracelet every time that plows furrows deep into your consciousness, making you aware of your behavior. When you recognize your complaints, you will begin to change.

Oh, and there is nothing magic about our Complaint Free bracelets. You can accomplish the same thing with a rubber band on your wrist or a coin in your pocket. The point is to physically move the rubber band to your other wrist or the coin to your other pocket every time you complain and begin anew at Day 1.

In this book, you'll learn why people complain, how complaining is destructive to our lives, the benefits (yes, benefits) people derive from complaining, the five reasons people complain, and even how to get others to stop complaining. Most important, you will learn the steps to eradicating this poisonous form of expression from your life.

As I mentioned, more than ten million Complaint Free bracelets have been sent out. Do I believe that every single person stayed with it until they went twenty-one consecutive days without complaining? No. I'm sure some of the bracelets ended up in a dusty corner of the recipient's drawer.

Diet books are perennial bestsellers because people buy them, try what is recommended for a while, and then when they discover the diet actually means they have to put forth effort and practice restraint, they stop. They have not changed their eating habits and soon gain back any weight they lost and more! Then they buy another diet book and the cycle continues.

You can read this book and give the whole bracelet thing

a try and then stop and give the next thing a try, or you can radically transform your life.

I once heard someone quip, "The worst thing about my home gym is remembering to dust it." He had purchased his expensive home exercise equipment from one of those late-night infomercials and never used it.

Let me repeat the words that opened this introduction: In your hands you hold the secret to transforming your life. Commit now that your Complaint Free bracelet won't end up in the back of a drawer the way most home exercise equipment ends up in the garage (one step closer to the Dumpster).

> "If I were to say, 'God, why me?' about the bad things, then I should have said, 'God, why me?' about the good things that happened in my life."
>
> —ARTHUR ASHE

Remember that your participation in this makes you part of a worldwide movement to improve the overall attitude of everyone in the world.

And it's working.

If you consider that the average person complains fifteen to thirty times a day, let's say an average of twenty-three complaints per person per day, and ten million Complaint Free bracelets have been sent out, even if only *half* of the people stay with it, that's one hundred fifteen million fewer complaints spoken around the world each and every day. *One hundred fifteen million!*

And, if you like math, consider that this means that 41,975,000,000 fewer complaints are spoken each year. If the digits throw you, that's nearly forty-two trillion fewer complaints each year. And we're only ten million bracelets toward our goal of sixty million.

Excited? You should be. You're part of a global transformation movement that is improving the lives of everyone. Now that you know about Complaint Free bracelets, you will begin to see them everywhere. One of our volunteers was in Amsterdam recently and saw college students wearing them.

I was at a Kansas City Royals game, and there was a group of fans trying desperately to get a "wave" going around the stadium. The wave would begin with great enthusiasm as people leapt to their feet, raised their arms, and let out a big "whoop!" The wave traveled around the park but faded every time it reached a certain section. The fans in that section, for whatever reason, were not committed to the wave and it stopped. The wave died.

This wave of human consciousness transformation has now been passed on to you. You can keep it going. You can help create a Complaint Free World.

Do it for your family. Do it for your nation. Do it for your children and their children yet to come. Do it because it's a powerful first step toward world peace.

"Okay," you're probably thinking, "world peace? Now you've crossed the line of believability." Well, consider this:

I received an e-mail from a nonprofit in Los Angeles that was handing out our Complaint Free bracelets to teenage gang members. The leader of the group e-mailed to say, "Gang violence always begins with one person complaining to or about someone in a rival gang. No complaints means no violence."

If it works for teenagers, it will work for countries.

So stay with it for all of these reasons. But most important, stay with it for yourself.

"Do this for myself?" you may be thinking. "Isn't that selfish?"

No.

There is nothing wrong with doing something so you will benefit. As you become a happier person, you raise the overall level of happiness in the world; you turn up the light and drive shadows from our collective darkness. You send out a vibration of optimism and hope that will resound with others and will compound exponentially.

Anthropologist Margaret Mead wrote, "Never doubt that a small group of thoughtful, committed citizens can change the world. Indeed, it is the only thing that ever has."

After five years, the ripple continues, and you're part of it.

Now, let's get started on a great new you . . .

PS: I've held back the ten millionth Complaint Free bracelet to give to the actor and rapper Will Smith. His philosophy of living, which I culled from interviews he has done and which appears in various YouTube videos, is an inspiring and shining example of how a person with single-minded focus and dogged determination will succeed every time.

How's this going to happen?

I don't know . . . but it's going to.

PART 1

UNCONSCIOUS INCOMPETENCE

I COMPLAIN THEREFORE I AM

Man invented language
to satisfy his deep need to complain.

−LILY TOMLIN

L ike most people, you spend much of your time swimming in a sea of negativity and complaints.

Just as a fish may not even be aware of the water that surrounds it, you may not be aware of all of the complaints you hear and speak. Complaining is so much a part of who we are, it's difficult to recognize what is and is not a complaint.

complain: to express grief, pain, or discontent

—MERRIAM-WEBSTER'S COLLEGIATE DICTIONARY

The Merriam-Webster dictionary defines "complain" as "to express grief, pain, or discontent."

By its very definition, a complaint is spoken. Some overzealous souls taking the twenty-one-day challenge have

> **VOICES**
>
> *Like most of the other folks who took up the Complaint Free Challenge, I quickly discovered exactly how many of the words I spoke in daily interactions were complaints. For the first time, I really heard myself when I vented about work, whined about my aches and pains, bemoaned political and world issues, and complained about the weather. What a shock to realize how many of my words held negative energy—and I considered myself such a positive person!*
>
> —MARTY POINTER,
>
> KANSAS CITY, MISSOURI

tried to switch their purple bracelet with every negative thought. The problem is that scientists estimate that we think about 70,000 thoughts every day. Trying to monitor each thought is futile. Consider a simpler, proven approach: Stop complaining and your thoughts will become more positive.

Think of your mind as a manufacturer and your mouth as a customer. The manufacturer produces negative thoughts that are purchased by the customer when they are expressed as complaints. It goes like this: The manufacturer (your brain) produces a negative thought, which the customer (your mouth) purchases by complaining. If the customer will stop buying what the manufacturer produces, the manufacturer will re-tool. When you stop complaining about what you perceive to be wrong and begin to speak about what you are grateful for and what you desire, you force your manufacturer brain to develop a new product line.

When you commit that what comes out of your mouth will be positive, your mind will become more aware of positive experiences to be used as raw materials to supply positive thoughts. As a result, the fundamental focus of your mind will shift. Your attention will be on what you want, and this is important: You will begin to draw more of what you want into your experience. Further, as you shift your focus away from the challenging aspects of life, you lessen their occurrence.

What you call reality will transform. This sounds simplistic, but it works. There is no reality, only perception. And you can change your perception.

> There is no reality, only perception. You can change your perception.

A complaint is distinguished from a statement of fact by the energy expressed. "It's hot today" is a statement of fact. A heavy sigh followed by the lament "It's hot today" is a complaint. In *A New Earth*, Eckhart Tolle summed it up this way,

Complaining is not to be confused with informing someone of a mistake or deficiency so that it can be put right. And to

refrain from complaining doesn't necessarily mean putting up with bad quality or behavior. There is no ego in telling the waiter your soup is cold and needs to be heated up—if you stick to the facts, which are always neutral. "How dare you serve me cold soup . . . ?" That's complaining.

There is negative energy being expressed with a complaint. Most complaints have a "This is unfair!" or "How dare this happen to me" quality. It's as if the complainer feels attacked by the actions of someone or something and counterattacks with complaints. Complaints are counterattacks for perceived injustices. A statement of fact is a neutral comment intended to inform (not berate) the listener.

Complaints are counterattacks for perceived injustices. A statement of fact is a neutral comment intended to inform (not berate) the listener.

A man from Bosnia e-mailed to say that, sadly, his country is famous worldwide for one thing: war. His intention is to make his country famous for being Complaint Free. "I have not yet made it twenty-one consecutive days without complaining," he said. "I seem to hit a wall around Day 4 and have to start over again, but I have found that I'm already a much happier person. . . . IS IT SUPPOSED TO DO THAT?"

I laughed out loud.

It's as if becoming a happier person while becoming Complaint Free is a side effect that we should have disclosed. Perhaps our website and my book jackets should carry a warning: "ATTENTION: ATTEMPTING TO BECOME COMPLAINT FREE MAY SPONTANEOUSLY INDUCE HAPPINESS!"

One of the most frequent comments we receive from people taking the Complaint Free challenge is that, long before they reach twenty-one consecutive days, they find that they do feel happier.

This happiness compounds on itself because happy people tend to attract more positive people, joyful experiences, and opportunities than do unhappy people. As a result, they feel even happier, which draws more good things, and this wonderful cycle continues and expands.

Researchers believe that there are four stages to becoming competent at anything. In becoming a Complaint Free person, you will go through each of these stages, and sorry, you can't skip steps. You can't race through or jump steps and effect lasting change. Depending on your experience, some of the stages may last longer than others. You might soar through one stage and then become stuck in another stage for a long time, but if you stay with it you will master the skill of being Complaint Free.

The four stages to competency are:

1. Unconscious Incompetence
2. Conscious Incompetence

3. Conscious Competence
4. Unconscious Competence

Right now, you are in the Unconscious Incompetence stage. You don't realize (are unconscious of) how much you complain (are incompetent). The average person may complain fifteen to thirty times a day, but you probably aren't aware of whether you are at the low end of the spectrum, the high end, or totally off the chart.

A woman getting out of bed in the middle of the night stubs her toe on a table leg. As the pain shoots up her body, she reflexively shouts, "Ouch!" It is normal to say "ouch" when we are hurt. Many people, however, are an "OUCH!" in search of a hurt. They walk around ouching about the difficulties and problems in their life and then are surprised when more of them show up. If you cry "ouch," the hurt will show up. If you complain, you'll receive more to complain about. It's the Law of Attraction in action. As you complete these stages, as you leave complaining behind, you will no longer be an "ouch" looking for a hurt. You will attract pleasure rather than pain.

In "Ode on a Distant Prospect of Eton College," Thomas Gray gave us the oft-quoted phrase "ignorance is bliss." As you become a Complaint Free person, you begin in the bliss of ignorance because you are unaware of how often you complain; you then move through the turmoil of awareness and transformation and finally arrive at true bliss.

Unconscious Incompetence is as much a state of being as a stage of competency.

This is where everyone begins his or her attempt to master any new skill. In Unconscious Incompetence you are pure potential, ready to create great things for yourself. There are exciting new vistas about to be explored. All you have to do is be willing to go through the remaining steps, which will make you a master at living a Complaint Free life and allow you to reap the many attendant rewards.

People ask, "Are you saying I can't complain *ever*?"

> "When any fit of gloominess, or perversion of mind, lays hold upon you, make it a rule not to publish it by complaints."
>
> —SAMUEL JOHNSON

To which I respond, "Of course you can complain." And I say this for two reasons:

1. I'm not out to tell you or anyone else what to do. If I were, I'd be trying to change you, and that means I'm focusing on something about you I don't like. I'd be expressing discontent about you and, by inference, complaining. So you can do whatever you want. It's your choice.
2. Sometimes it makes sense to complain.

Now, before you feel you've found your loophole in number 2 above, consider that word "sometimes" and remember that I and thousands of people around the world have gone twenty-one consecutive days, that's three solid weeks in a row, or 504 back-to-back hours, without complaining at all. No Complaints, zero, zip! When it comes to complaining, "sometimes" means "not very often at all."

If we are honest with ourselves, life events that lead us to express grief, pain, or discontent are *exceptionally* rare. Certainly there are individuals around the world who are facing very difficult lives, and everyone goes through hard times here and there.

However, many people today are living in the safest, healthiest, and most prosperous time in all of human history. And yet what do they do? They complain.

This is not new. Hundreds of years ago, Benjamin Franklin said, "Constant complaint is the poorest sort of pay for all the comforts we enjoy." When Franklin wrote this, there was no electricity, aspirin, penicillin, air-conditioning, indoor plumbing, air travel, or many more of the thousands of modern niceties and so-called necessities we now take for granted. Nonetheless, he felt that his contemporaries were far too cavalier about how good they had it. Franklin's generation had much less than we do, and yet we, like them, still find ample reasons to complain.

> "Constant complaint is the poorest sort of pay for all the comforts we enjoy."
>
> —BEN FRANKLIN

Little if any of the complaining we do is calculated to improve our situation. It's just a lot of "ear pollution," detrimental to our happiness and well-being.

Check yourself. When you complain (express grief, pain, or discontent), is the cause severe? Are you complaining frequently? Or are you an "ouch" looking for a hurt?

To be a happy person living life by design, you need a very, very high threshold for what leads you to expressing grief, pain, and discontent. The next time you're about to complain about something, ask yourself how your situation stacks up to something that happened to me.

I was sitting in my home office, writing. The home my family lived in at the time was located at a sharp bend in the road. Drivers had to slow down to take the curve, but just two hundred yards past our house the city road became a county highway and the speed limit jumped from 25 mph to 55 mph. Because of the curve and the lower speed limit, cars would slow down to a crawl in front of our house and then accelerate rapidly heading out of town. Or they'd race into town and brake quickly just in front of our house to make the curve. If it weren't for that curve, the road in front of our home would have been in a very dangerous place.

It was a warm spring afternoon and the lace curtains flapped rhythmically in the breeze. Suddenly I heard a sound that snapped me from work: a loud *thud* followed by a scream. The scream was not that of a person but rather an animal.

Every animal, just like every person, has a unique voice, and I knew this voice well. It was our long-haired golden retriever, Ginger.

Normally we don't think of dogs screaming. Barking, howling, whimpering—yes; but not screaming. Nonetheless, that's exactly what Ginger was doing. She had been crossing the road in front of our house, and a vehicle had hit her. She lay in the road shrieking with pain not twenty feet outside my window. I shouted and ran through the living room and out the front door, followed by my daughter Lia. Lia was six years old at the time.

As we approached Ginger, we could tell she was badly injured. She was using her front legs to try and stand, but her hind legs did not seem capable of helping. Over and over she yowled in pain. Neighbors poured from their homes to see what was causing the commotion. Lia stood frozen and just kept saying her name, "Ginger . . . Ginger . . . ," as the tears flowed down her cheeks and wet her shirt.

I looked around for the driver who had hit Ginger but saw no one. Then I saw a truck towing a trailer headed out of town, cresting the hill, and accelerating well past 55 mph. Even though our dog lay there in agony and my daughter cried piteously, I was consumed with confronting the person who had hit Ginger. "How could anyone do this and just drive off?" I said angrily. "He had to slow down to come around the curve. . . . Surely he saw her, surely he knew what happened!"

I jumped into my car and fishtailed out of the driveway, leaving a plume of dust and gravel. Sixty, seventy-five, then eighty-three miles per hour along the uneven road, in pursuit of the person who had hit Lia's dog and left without so much as facing us. I was going so fast on the uncertain surface that my car began to feel as if it were floating tenuously above the ground. In that moment, I calmed myself enough to realize that if I were killed while driving, it would be even harder on everyone than Ginger's having been hurt. I slowed just enough to control my car as the distance between me and other driver narrowed.

Having turned into his driveway, and not realizing I was chasing him, the driver stepped out of his truck in a torn shirt and dirty jeans. His greasy baseball cap, which sported a profane witticism, was pushed back on his sunburned forehead. I skidded in behind him and jumped from my car screaming, "You hit my dog!" The man turned and looked at me quizzically as if I had spoken to him in a foreign language.

With the blood raging in my ears, I wasn't sure I heard him correctly when he said, "I know I hit your dog. . . . What are you going to do about it?"

It took a moment for the shock of his comment to wear off. After regaining my connection with reality, I stammered, "Wh-*what*? What did you say?" He smiled as if correcting an errant child and then said again, slowly and deliberately, "I know I hit your dog. . . . What exactly are you going to do about it?"

I went blind with rage. In my mind I saw the image of Lia's slumped shoulders in my rearview mirror as she stood sobbing over Ginger's body writhing in pain.

I yelled, "Put up your hands."

"What?" he asked, grinning sarcastically.

"Put up your hands," I said again. "Defend yourself. . . . I'm going to kill you!"

A few moments ago, reason had kept me from killing myself while driving in a white-hot rage to find this guy. Now his dismissive and cavalier comment about having hurt, possibly mortally wounded, our beloved Ginger had vanquished all reason.

I had never been in a fight in my adult life. I don't believe in fighting. I wasn't sure I knew how to fight. But I wanted to beat this man to death. I was insane with anger. I didn't care if I ended up in prison.

"I ain't gonna fight you," he said. "And if you hit me, it's assault, mister."

I stood there dumbfounded, my arms raised, my fists clenched hard as diamonds.

"Fight me!" I demanded.

"No, sir," he said through his remaining teeth. "I ain't gonna do no such thing. And if you hit me, it's assault."

He turned his back and lumbered slowly away. I stood shaking, anger poisoning my blood.

I don't remember driving home. I don't remember lifting Ginger up and taking her to the veterinarian's office. I do remember the way she smelled the last time I held her and the way she whimpered softly as the vet's needle ended her suffering. "How could a person do such a thing?" I asked, choking back bitter tears.

Days later the man's jagged smile still haunted me as I tried to sleep. His "I know I hit your dog, what are you going to do about it?" rang in my ears. I visualized exactly what I would have done to him had we fought. In my visions I was a superhero destroying an evil villain. Sometimes I imagined I had a baseball bat or other weapon and was hurting him; hurting him badly, hurting him as he had hurt me, Lia, and Ginger.

On the third night of unsuccessful attempts to sleep, I got up and began to write in my journal. After spilling out my grief, pain, and discontent for nearly an hour, I wrote something surprising: "Those who hurt are hurting." Taking in my words as if they were from someone else, I said aloud "What?"

Again my pen wrote, "Those who hurt are hurting." I sat back brooding in my chair and listened to the crickets celebrating the spring night. "Those who hurt are hurting? What does that have to do with this guy?"

As I thought more about it, I began to understand. A person

who could so easily hurt a treasured family pet must not know the love of companion animals as we do. A person who can drive away while a young child folds into tears could not fully know the love of children. A man who refuses to apologize for spearing a family's heart must have had his own heart speared many, many times. This man was the real victim in this story. Truly he had acted as a villain, but it came as a result of the depth of pain within him.

I sat a long time letting this all sink in. Every time I began to feel angry with him and the pain he caused, I thought of the pain this man must live with on a daily basis. After a while, I noticed my breathing slowing down, my tension relaxing. I switched off the light, went to bed, and slept soundly.

complain: to express grief, pain, or discontent

During this experience I felt **grief**. Ginger had shown up five years prior at our home in rural South Carolina. Several stray dogs had appeared at our home over the years, but our dog Gibson always ran them off. For some reason, Ginger he let stay. There was something special about Ginger. We presumed from her demeanor that she had been abused prior to coming to live with us. And, because she especially shied away from me, it was probably a man who had mistreated her. Tentatively, after a year or so, she had begun to trust me. And in the remaining years she had become a true friend. I deeply grieved her passing.

I certainly felt **pain**, real emotional pain that tore at my soul. Those of us with children know that we would rather endure any pain than have our children hurt. And the pain my Lia was going through redoubled my own.

I felt **discontent**. I felt torn for not having thrashed the guy, as well as for having considered acting violently in the first place. I felt ashamed for walking away from him and equally ashamed for having chased after him in the first place.

Grief. Pain. Discontent.

When this man hit Ginger, it was appropriate for me to have felt and to have expressed each of these. You may have experienced something equally difficult at some time in your life. Fortunately, such traumatic events are rare. Similarly, complaining (expressing grief, pain, or discontent) should be rare.

But for most people, our complaints are not sourced by such deeply painful experiences. Rather we're like the character in the Joe Walsh song "Life's Been Good"—we can't complain, but sometimes, in fact many times, we still do. Things are not really bad enough to warrant expressing grief, pain, or discontent, but complaining is our default setting. It's simply habitual; it's what we do.

Prior to beginning your trek down the path to becoming a

Complaint Free person, you were probably blissfully unaware of how much you complain and the damaging effect of your complaints on your life. For many, griping about the weather, their spouse, their work, their bodies, their friends, their jobs, the economy, other drivers, their country, or whatever they are thinking about is something done dozens of times each and every day.

Few realize how often they complain. The words come out of their mouths, so their ears must hear them. But, for some reason, the words don't register as complaints. It seems that complaining is like bad breath—we notice it when it comes out of someone else's mouth but not when it comes from our own.

> Complaining is like bad breath. We notice it when it comes out of someone else's mouth, but not when it comes out of our own.

Chances are you complain a lot more than you think. And now that you've accepted the twenty-one-day challenge to become Complaint Free, you have begun to notice it. As you start moving the bracelet from wrist to wrist, you will realize how much you kvetch (Yiddish for "complain habitually").

Up until this point, you would probably have said, honestly, that you don't complain—much, anyway. Certainly you think that you only complain when something is legitimately bothering you. The next time you're tempted to rationalize your complaining, remember Ginger's story and ask yourself if what you're going through is that bad. Then resolve to keep your commitment to become Complaint Free.

Everyone who has become a Twenty-One-Day Complaint Free Champion has said to me, "It wasn't easy, but it was worth it." Nothing valuable is ever easy. Simple? Yes. But "easy" is not part of becoming a successful person. I say this not to discourage you but

> "If at first you don't succeed, you're running about average."
>
> —M. H. ALDERSON

to inspire you. If you find becoming a Complaint Free person (monitoring and changing your words) difficult, it doesn't mean that you can't do it. And it doesn't mean there is something wrong with you. M. H. Alderson said, "If at first you don't succeed, you're running about average." If you're complaining, you're right where you're supposed to be. Now you're becoming aware of it and you can begin to erase it from your life.

Just switch your bracelet with each complaint and start again.

Recently, Lia, now age fifteen, and I drove to Alexandria, Indiana, to meet Mike Carmichael and his wife Glenda. Mike works as a painting contractor, and four decades ago he had a unique idea. He drilled a hole through a regulation baseball, threaded a coat hanger through the ball and then dipped it in a bucket of paint. When he returned home the next day, he dipped the ball again. Whenever Mike would come home from work, he would dip the ball in the paint left over from his day's work and hang it up to dry. Each time he immersed the ball, he kept a record of how many coats covered it.

When he reached one thousand coats of paint, his little experiment had taken on the size and oblong shape of a bottle of bleach. Mike was fascinated by how a single coat of paint, which measures only five one-hundredths of an inch in thickness, applied every single day would ultimately grow something so large.

In 1977, Mike decided to take his idea to another level. He took a fresh baseball, drilled a much larger hole, and inserted a thick metal hook. He hung the ball in his workshop and invited family, friends, and passersby to apply a coat of paint to the ball. Today, a sign hangs in front of his workshop boasting the "World's Largest Ball of Paint."

Lia and I pulled into Mike's driveway. As we entered the room where the ball resides, we saw that it now hangs from steel girders. Mike stood proudly next to his creation, and I gasped at the enormity of the thing.

I asked Mike how much it weighs. He said that several months ago he had used a crane to hoist it onto the back of a truck so it could be weighed on the scales used to weigh tractor-trailers. Major League Baseball says that an official baseball should weigh 5.25 ounces. This baseball, now covered in tens of thousands of coats of paint, each not much thicker than a human hair, tipped the scales at an astounding 3,500 pounds! I was dumbfounded. After a moment I asked, "How big is it?"

MLB standard is that a regulation baseball must be between two and seven-eighths and three inches in diameter. Without paint, this is the size of Mike's baseball. Mike handed one end of a carpenter's measuring tape to Glenda, and they stretched it out for us to see. "Just over fifty-two inches in diameter," he said, with a smile that seemed as wide as the ball of paint itself.

The number 22,799 was written in red across the front of the ball.

"What does 22,799 represent?" Lia asked.

"That's the coat of paint you and your dad are going to apply today," Mike said.

"Really?" Lia asked excitedly.

"Absolutely," said Mike. "What color do you want to use?"

Lia and I smiled at each other. "Purple!" we said simultaneously.

Minutes later, Mike handed each of us a paint roller soaked in purple paint. Working diligently, it took the two of us about fifteen minutes to evenly coat the mammoth ball. While we were painting, Mike asked, "What brings you two here?"

I pointed to the purple Complaint Free bracelet on my right wrist and told Mike about the more than ten million people around the world who have taken the challenge. We then talked about habits.

"Habits direct our lives," I said. "We do so many things simply because they are things we have done over and over. What starts out as a single event, just like a single coat of paint on a three-inch baseball, will, over time, become something massive, just like this one-and-three-quarter-ton ball of paint."

> "Habits are formed by the repetition of particular acts. They are strengthened by an increase in the number of repeated acts. Habits are also weakened or broken, and contrary habits are formed by the repetition of contrary acts."
>
> —MORTIMER ADLER

Mike thought a moment and said he'd never thought of the correlation before, but it made a lot of sense. As we were leaving, Mike handed me a small curio to take with me. To keep the massive ball round, he must occasionally shear off drips that form on the bottom of the ball. The piece he handed me was about as wide as a silver dollar and about as thick as a pencil. As I looked at this sliver shaved from the World's Largest Ball of Paint, I could see the hundreds of paper-thin individual coats that had created its hulking girth.

American philosopher, author, and educator Mortimer

Adler wrote, "Habits are formed by the repetition of particular acts. They are strengthened by an increase in the number of repeated acts. Habits are also weakened or broken, and contrary habits are formed by the repetition of contrary acts." For most people, complaining is a habit that has been reinforced time and again through repetition. However, if you consciously strive not to complain, in time you will no longer default to this mode of expression.

Not expressing a single complaint seems like it may not have much of an impact on your life, but it begins to stem the tide of the complaining habit that has defined who you are. As you bite your tongue and swallow back a complaint, you are adding a coat of paint to a new habit that will take on momentum and grow to define the new you.

You may doubt that you can go twenty-one consecutive days without complaining, but you *can*. I complained dozens of times every single day, and I made it. The key is not to give up. I know a wonderful elderly woman who is still wearing one of the original purple bracelets we gave out. It's now tattered and gray, but she says dogmatically, "They might bury me in this thing but I'm not giving up."

That's the level of commitment it takes. Commit to never giving up. Remember the good news that even before you make twenty-one consecutive days of not complaining, you will find your internal focus shifting and yourself becoming happier. Here's an e-mail I received:

Hi,

Like thousands, I have already begun changing my focus. While waiting for my bracelet, I have started to wear a rubber band around my wrist. This has made me aware of what I'm doing. I've been doing this for about a week, and I am now rarely complaining. <u>The remarkable thing about this is how much happier I feel!</u> Not to mention how much happier those around me must be (like my husband!). I have wanted to work on my complaining for a long time and the bracelet campaign has been the impetus for my changing behavior.

The subject of the bracelets and the mission behind them has come up in MANY conversations, so the mission has a HUGE ripple effect where MANY people are at least thinking about how often they complain and perhaps deciding to behave differently. This movement may have a very far-reaching effect as more and more people hear of the idea. The reach of this mission is far greater than those who actually get the bracelets! Awesome to think about!

JEANNE REILLY

ROCKVILLE, MARYLAND

Venerated radio commentator Paul Harvey once said, "I hope one day to achieve enough of what the world calls success so that if someone asks me how I did it I will tell them,

'I get up more times than I fall.'" As with all things worth accomplishing, to become Complaint Free you must fail your way to success. If you're like most, when you begin this process, you will probably move your bracelet from arm to arm until you get sore and tired of doing it. I moved my bracelet so many times that I broke three of them before making it twenty-one consecutive days. If you break yours, go to www .AComplaintFreeWorld.org and order more.

If you'll stay with it, one day you'll be in lying in bed about to drift off to sleep, and you'll glance at your wrist. There, for the first time in days or possibly weeks, you'll see that your purple bracelet is on the same wrist as when you got out of bed that morning. You'll think, "I must have complained at some point today and just not caught myself." But as you do a mental inventory, you'll realize that you made it. You actually made it one whole day without complaining! One day at a time. You can do it.

As you begin this transformation, you are fortunate because even with my reminding you of the difficulty ahead, you have a psychological advantage working for you. It's called the Dunning-Kruger effect. The Dunning-Kruger effect is named for David Dunning and Justin Kruger of Cornell University, who did studies on people attempting to learn new skills. Whenever a person tries something new, be it skiing, juggling, playing the flute, riding a horse, meditating, writing a book, painting a picture, or anything else, it is part of human nature to think it will be simple to master. Dunning and Kruger's results, published in the December 1999 *Journal of Personality and Social Psychology*, stated, "Ignorance more frequently begets confidence than does knowledge." In other words, you're not aware that doing something is difficult, so you give it a try. You think, "This is going to be easy," so you begin, and getting started is always the most difficult part.

Without the Dunning-Kruger effect, if you knew the amount of effort it would actually take to become proficient at a new skill, you would probably give up before you began.

Begin now to wear the purple bracelet (or wear the rubber band, put the coin in your pocket, or use some other self-monitoring tool) and move it with every complaint. Move it, even though it seems hard, embarrassing, or frustrating. Move it, even after you've made it ten days, complained, and have to start over again. Start over again and again. Stay with it even if others around you have given up. Stay with it even if others around you have succeeded and your personal best so far is only a couple of days.

> Complaining keeps our focus on the problem at hand rather than the resolution sought.

At the beginning of this chapter, I shared the dictionary definition of "complain." Over the last several years I have developed my own definition: *A complaint is an energetic statement that focuses on the problem at hand rather than the resolution sought.*

A complaint has energy, typically "How dare this happen to me?" energy, behind it. And the biggest problem with complaining is that it keeps our focus on what is wrong, so that we don't even consider the ways a situation might be improved.

There is an old story of two construction workers sitting down to eat lunch together. The first worker opens his lunch box and complains, "Yech! A meat loaf sandwich. . . . I hate meat loaf sandwiches." His friend says nothing. The following day, the two meet up again for lunch. Again the first man opens his lunch box, looks inside, and, this time more agitated, says, "Another meat loaf sandwich? I hate meat loaf sandwiches!" As before, his colleague remains silent. The third day, the two men gather for lunch, and the first construction worker opens his lunch box and stomps about and shouts, "I've had it! Day in and day out, it's the same thing! Meat loaf sandwiches every blessed day! I want something else!"

His friend asks, "Why don't you just ask your wife to make you something else?"

With true bewilderment on his face, the first worker replies, "I make my own lunch."

You, me, and everyone else—we all make our own lunch. We create our lives with our thoughts, and our words broadcast what we are thinking. Remember the line from the song "Already Gone" by the Eagles: "So oftentimes it happens that we live our lives in chains, and we never even know we have the key." You are chained to the meat loaf sandwich menu, and you are the one holding the key.

> "So oftentimes it happens that we live our lives in chains, and we never even know we have the key."
>
> —THE EAGLES,
> "ALREADY GONE"

A friend related a real-life version of this meat loaf sandwich story. Over coffee he told me that two years ago his company had changed their voice mail system. Rather than punching in codes and directions via the telephone keypad to retrieve voice mails, all the employees now would have to do is pick up the receiver and say, "Get messages," then speak commands such as "Replay message" or "Delete message."

"That's what's *supposed* to happen," he told me. "The problem is that sometimes the system doesn't work very well, and if there is any background noise or if we aren't crystal clear in what we say, the system either doesn't respond or does the wrong thing."

He went on to tell me about a woman in the next cubicle who often has trouble retrieving her messages. If she says, "Get messages," and the system doesn't respond or does the wrong thing, she will shout, *"Get messages, dammit!"* Of course, the expletive after the command further confounds the automated attendant, ensuring that instead of her messages the woman gets a meat loaf sandwich.

"She's yelling at a machine," my friend said with a bemused smile. "And her anger makes the problem worse." After a sip of coffee he added, "Now here's the really sad part. When they installed the new phone system twenty-four months ago, I realized that the voice recognition feature didn't work well, so I went into the settings and changed my phone back to manual input. I touch the keys just like before to get my messages.

"When I heard this woman yelling into her receiver, I told her that her voice mail could be changed back to manual input. She was screeching into her phone, *'Get messages, you worthless piece of crap!'* and, without even looking my way, sniped: 'I'm too busy right now, I'll do it later!'"

My friend shook his head. "That was two years ago," he said. "I've offered a dozen times to help her change it back, and every time she says she's 'too busy.' I told her it takes less than thirty seconds to fix, but she keeps refusing my help. She doesn't have time to fix the problem, but she's wasted hours over the last couple of years yelling into the phone.

"Can you imagine?" he continued. "She comes into work *every single day* knowing that she is going to wrestle with the voice mail system. She knows she can fix it in less than a minute, and yet does nothing. Astounding!"

Are you tired of meat loaf sandwiches? You're making your own lunch each and every day. Your thoughts create your life, and your words indicate what you are thinking. Change what you are saying, and your thoughts will change, your life will improve.

When Jesus said, "Seek and ye shall find," it was a statement of universal principle. What you seek, you will find. When you complain, you are using the incredible power of your mind to seek out things that you profess not to want but that you nonetheless draw to you time and again. Then, when they show up, you complain about these new things and attract still more of what you don't want. You get caught in the "complaint loop"—a self-fulfilling prophecy of complaint > negative experience, complaint > negative experience, complaint > negative experience, and on and on it goes.

In *The Outsider*, Albert Camus wrote, "Gazing up at the dark sky spangled with its signs and stars, for the first time, I laid my heart open to the benign indifference of the universe." The Universe is benign indifference. The Universe, or God, or Spirit, or whatever you choose to call it is benign (good), but it is also indifferent (it does not care). The Universe doesn't care if you use the power of your thoughts as indicated by your words to attract love, health, happiness, abundance, and peace, or to invite pain, suffering, misery, loneliness, and poverty. Our thoughts create our lives; our words indicate what we are thinking. When we control our words by eradicating complaining, we create our lives with intention and attract what we desire.

In Chinese, the word "complain" is composed of two symbols, "hug" and "ego." The Chinese believe that to complain is to "hug your ego." There is profound wisdom in the pairing of these two signs to indicate the essence of complaining. When you complain you are hugging your ego.

The ego referred to is not from the Freudian concept of the three-part psychological makeup of human beings. Rather, it is the concept of the limited human self that feels it is cut off from infinite supply.

When you complain, you hug your ego. You provide aid, comfort, and validation to that strident voice in your head that insists you do not deserve what you desire, that limited self that feels cut off from the abundance of the world. You limit your ability to enjoy affluence.

The word "affluent" means "to be in the abundant flow." There is a cascading river of goodness flowing at all times. When you complain, you divert the course of the flow around you. When you begin to speak only of what you desire, you allow the flow to wash over you, drenching you with all manner of goodness.

When you begin to attempt to eradicate complaining from

your life, you have years of this habit pushing you toward failure. It's like being on a jet traveling north at six hundred miles per hour. If the pilot turns the jet westward, you will feel your body straining to the right because you have been moving with great speed in that direction. If the jet stays true to its new course, you will soon settle in and no longer feel the pull of your previous direction.

Similarly, your previous habits will pull you when you attempt to change them. As you stay with your commitment to switch your Complaint Free bracelet, you will feel a strong pull to resort back to your negative ways. Keep going. Each passing moment and each switch of the bracelet is a single coat of paint that adds to what will soon swell into a mighty force and transform your life.

CHAPTER 2

COMPLAINING AND HEALTH

*Of all the self-fulfilling prophecies in our culture,
the assumption that aging means decline and
poor health is probably the deadliest.*

—MARILYN FERGUSON, *THE AQUARIAN CONSPIRACY*

We complain for the same reason we do anything: We perceive a benefit from doing so. I remember vividly the night I discovered the benefits of complaining. I was only thirteen years old and was attending my first dance, a sock hop. If you're too young to remember, sock hops were often held in high school gyms, and the kids were required to remove their shoes to protect the gymnasium floors. These dances were popular in the United States during the 1950s, but a resurgence of sock hops occurred with the 1973 release of the movie *American Graffiti*.

No single physical and emotional change is as impactful and lasting as becoming a teenager. As a thirteen-year-old boy, I discovered for the first time that girls were no longer "gross."

VOICES

I came home from work early yesterday and was having an exceptionally tough day with my back (major spinal fusion/cervical fusions). I just wanted to relax and feel sorry for myself. At forty-seven, I have a laundry list of medical issues that weigh me down. But when I plopped on the couch and watched you on Oprah, I was inspired! They say that eyes are the window to one's soul, and Will Bowen has the most amazing eyes! I was transfixed and not in an "icky" way! haha They twinkle and made me smile.

I complain every day about my pain and am on so many pain medications. You are right, the complaints do weigh me down, and I want to participate in the no complaint zone. I have ordered 10 bracelets for myself, and some friends. I am writing to you to say thank you.

I am most grateful to God that I CAN walk; I have good friends, a loving family, and a good job. I need to refocus my energies on being grateful and not wallow in self-pity for my myriad of medical problems. Thank you from the bottom of my heart and I can only hope that one day I can say thank you in person. You are inspiring, and like I said your eyes made me smile, and give me hope. God Bless you.

—CINDY LAFOLLETT,
CAMBRIDGE, OHIO

Suddenly girls were magnetically alluring and simultaneously terrifying. Terrifying as they might be, they nonetheless occupied my every waking thought and haunted my dreams. Thoughts of baseball, model ships, movies, and comics were all swept aside by images of girls.

I wanted desperately to connect with girls but had no idea how or what I'd do if I did. I was like the old joke about a dog chasing cars that finally caught one and didn't know what to do with it. I simultaneously craved being close to girls and feared going near them.

The night of the sock hop was a typical hot and humid South Carolina evening. Keeping with the 1950s theme, the girls wore poodle skirts, bouffant hairdos, saddle shoes, and bright red lipstick. The boys' costumes consisted primarily of peg leg jeans rolled up at the ankles, white socks, a pack of cigarettes (borrowed from our parents) rolled up in the sleeve of a white T-shirt, penny loafers with pennies in them, and hair slicked back into a DA (ducktail).

As hit songs from the 1950s filled the air, the girls stood giggling on one side of the gym while we guys lounged on metal folding chairs on the opposite side trying desperately to look cool. We acted aloof and in control but were actually panic-stricken by the thought of going over and talking to the girls, even though every strand of our DNA begged us to do so. "Let 'em come to us," we joked. If they did, our male pride would swell; and if not, at least they might think we didn't care.

My best friend at the time was Chip. Chip was tall, a good student, and a great athlete. Of the three I was, well, tall. Unlike Chip, I was quite chubby. When I was a teen, shopping for clothes meant a trip to the dimly lit basement of Belk's department store to rummage through the selection of "husky" (overweight boys') clothes.

Because he was tall and athletic, I could tell that several of the girls were eying Chip. I don't know which bothered me more: the girls' obvious attraction to Chip or his unwillingness to act on it. He just sat there, even though we encouraged him to get the dance started by going over and talking to the ponytailed and bobby-socked enchantresses who sat waiting for us to make the first move.

"I'm too shy," Chip said. "I don't know what to say."

"Just go over there; let them do the talking," I said. "You can't just sit here all night."

"*You're* just sitting here," said Chip. "You're Mr. Talkative. Why don't *you* go over and say something to them?"

Drug addicts will often remember the first time they tried what would ultimately become known as their "drug of choice," the narcotic that would consume and possibly even destroy their lives if they couldn't shake their addiction. With my next sentence, I was about to embark on an addiction to complaining that would last more than thirty years.

I leaned toward Chip and said, "Even if I went over there,

none of them would dance with me. Look at me—I'm too fat. I'm thirteen, and I shot past two hundred pounds a long time ago. I wheeze when I talk. I sweat when I walk."

Noticing the other boys looking at me, I continued, "Chip, you're in great shape. The girls are looking at you, not me." The other guys nodded in agreement. "I'm just a funny guy they like to talk to, but they don't want to dance with me. They don't want me . . . and they never will."

At that moment, another good friend walked up from behind and slapped me on the back. "Hey, fat boy!" he said.

Normally, his greeting would have meant nothing. Nearly everyone called me "fat boy." It was a nickname that suited me and one that I'd grown accustomed to. I never took it as an insult. These were my friends, and it didn't matter to them that I was fat. But when I was called "fat boy" after having just given a greatly embellished speech using my being overweight as an excuse to not ask a girl to dance, the effect on our little circle was palpable.

One of my guys glared at the one who called me fat boy and said, "Hey, shut up!"

"Leave him alone!" said another.

"It's not his fault he's fat!" a third interjected.

I looked round the circle as all my young friends looked at me with great concern.

After a moment's pause, the voice inside my head shouted,

"Play it up!" So I sighed dramatically and slowly looked away. We were all seeking escape routes to take us away from having to face and possibly be rejected by the girls. Chip's was being shy. Mine was being overweight. The combination of my complaining about being fat coupled with the timing of a playful insult from one of my friends not only had gotten me off the hook but also had led to attention and sympathy.

I had complained and in so doing had excused myself from doing something that frightened me, *and* I had also received attention, support, and validation. My drug had kicked in. I had found my addiction. Complaining could get me high.

Years later, when another friend and I applied for two jobs at a restaurant and my friend got the better shift, I told myself and others it was because I was fat. "Oh, that's not true, you're great!" I enjoyed being told. When I got a traffic ticket, I said it was because I was fat and people clicked their tongues in contempt at the police officer. It would take me another five and a half years to shed this pet excuse, as well as the one hundred extra pounds that were damaging my health.

In "Complaints and Complaining: Functions, Antecedents, and Consequences," published in the *Psychological Bulletin,* psychologist Robin Kowalski wrote, "Many complaints involve attempts to elicit particular interpersonal reactions from others, such as sympathy or approval. For example, people may complain about their health, not because they actually feel sick but because the *sick role* allows them to achieve secondary gains such as sympathy from others or the avoidance of aversive events."

By complaining and playing the "fat" card, I had gotten sympathy and approval, and I had expressed a justifiable reason for not talking to the girls. My complaining had benefited me. Chances are you have done something similar. You may have complained about your health to get sympathy or attention and/or to avoid stepping up to do something you were afraid of doing. The problem with complaining about our health is that it tends to draw to us the actual experience of sickness. What goes into your mouth determines the size and shape of your body. What comes out of your mouth determines your reality.

> "Many complaints involve attempts to elicit particular interpersonal reactions from others, such as sympathy or approval."
>
> —DR. ROBIN KOWALSKI

> What goes into your mouth determines the size and shape of your body. What comes out of your mouth determines your reality.

In my speeches I've asked tens of thousands of people to raise their hands if they know someone who complains frequently about his or her health. "Now," I say, "keep your hands up if this person who complains about their poor health actually tends to be sick often." Typically, 99 percent of the hands stay up.

Poor health is one of the most common complaints people voice. People complain about their health to play the sick role so as to derive sympathy and attention and to avoid events they are averse to, such as adopting a healthier lifestyle. Certainly there are some who complain who do have poor health, but even this keeps focus on their struggles, making those struggles more prevalent in their lives.

In *Happiness for Dummies*, Dr. W. Doyle Gentry tells of a man who lives with chronic pain as a result of an accident. The man has explored every conceivable path to relieve his suffering, but there are times when his pain is unmanageable and unbearable. The man's solution is to engage in something that takes his focus away from the pain. Doyle writes that the man will sit in front of his computer and read anything and everything that interests him. With his focus off his pain, the severity of the pain lessens.

People who complain about their pain are not only notifying the world as to their suffering but are also reminding their own bodies to look for and experience pain.

People often say to me, "Oh, so you're saying I should fake it till I make it."

No.

There is no such thing as "fake it till you make it." As pithy as this trite little rhyme is, it is not applicable to personal transformation. As soon as you begin acting like the person you wish to become, you *are* that person. The first step to being different is to act like the person you aspire to become. It is the first step toward self-mastery. To trivialize this most important of actions by calling it "faking it" misses the point.

You're not faking it. You are *being* it, even if only momentarily, and even if only in a limited way compared to your ideal.

> "We cannot become what we want to be by remaining the way we are."
>
> —MAX DE PREE

Life is not static. Life is a constant shift. When you are sick, you're either getting sicker or getting better. When I was grossly obese as a teen, my actions either took me toward becoming more fit and healthy or moved me toward being out of shape. As soon as I changed my diet, I was the thin, healthy person I wanted to be even if it took many months for my body to reflect the new me.

Ask yourself, "Have I ever played the sick role? Am I doing it now?" When you complain about your health, you may receive sympathy and attention, but the price you pay is perpetuating your misery.

You have probably heard of someone experiencing psychosomatic illness. When we hear the term "psychosomatic," we tend to think of a neurotic sick person whose illness has no physiological basis.

Psychosomatic comes from *psycho*, meaning "mind," and

soma, meaning "body." Therefore, psychosomatic literally means "mind/body." We are all psychosomatic because we are all a unified expression of our minds and our bodies.

According to Dr. Robin Kowalski, medical doctors estimate that nearly two-thirds of their time is spent treating patients whose illnesses have psychological origins.

> "If you have headache, or sciatica, or leprosy, or thunderstroke, I beseech you, by all angels, to hold your peace and not pollute the morning."
>
> —RALPH WALDO EMERSON

Think about that. *Two-thirds* of most illnesses originate in or are made worse by our minds. What the mind believes, the body manifests. Dozens of research studies have shown that what a person believes about his or her health leads to that belief becoming real.

A recent story on National Public Radio detailed a study wherein doctors found that if they told patients a particular drug held great promise in curing them, the drug had a far more beneficial effect than it did on patients who received the same drug without such a suggestion. The story went on to report that Alzheimer's patients who had other physical challenges, such as high blood pressure, did not get the full benefit of the drugs they took for those challenges because, due to their diminished memory, they could not remember taking their daily medications. The mind has a powerful effect on the body.

I was once called upon to visit a woman I will call Jane, who was in the hospital. Before I entered Jane's room, I stopped at the nurses' station to ask the doctor about Jane's condition.

"She's fine," said the doctor. "She's had a stroke, but she'll recover fully."

I knocked at Jane's door, and a weak voice responded haltingly, "Who is it?"

"Jane?" I said, "It's Will Bowen."

Entering Jane's room, I questioned the doctor's report. Jane looked to be anything but "fine." She repeated, "Who is it?"

"It's Will Bowen," I said warmly. And then to jog her memory, I added, "Your minister." At that time, I was serving as senior minister of a church in Kansas City, Missouri.

"Oh, thank God you're here," she said. "I'm dying."

"You're what?" I asked.

"I'm dying. I've only got a few days. I'm glad you're here so we can plan my funeral."

"If you keep saying things are going to be bad, you have a chance of being a prophet."

—ISAAC BASHEVIS SINGER

At that moment, the doctor entered to check on Jane, and I pulled her aside. "I thought you said she was going to be okay," I said.

"She is," said the doctor.

"But she just told me she's dying," I said.

Rolling her eyes in exasperation, the doctor walked over to stand beside Jane's bed. "Jane? Jane!" she said.

Jane opened her eyes. "You've had a stroke, hon', you're not dying," said the doctor. "You're going to be okay. Just a few more days here in Intensive Care and we'll move you into Rehab. You'll be home with your cat Marty in no time, okay?"

A weak smile crossed Jane's face. "Okay," she whispered.

When the doctor had left the room, Jane turned her gaze toward me and said, "Can you get a pen and a piece of paper, please?"

"What for?" I asked

"We've got to plan my funeral," she said. "I'm dying."

"But you're not dying!" I protested. "I'll make notes, and when you die—a long time from now—then I can do your funeral."

Jane slowly shook her head, "I'm dying now." And she proceeded to detail her wishes for her memorial service.

On my way out, I talked to the doctor again. "She's convinced she's dying," I said.

She smiled. "Look, we're all going to die someday, even Jane. But she's only had a stroke, and it's not going to kill her. She's going to recover fully, with no lingering aftereffects."

Two weeks later, I officiated at Jane's funeral.

It didn't matter what her doctor said; Jane was convinced that she was dying, and her body believed her and responded to that belief.

When you complain about your health, you are putting out

negative statements that your body hears. Your complaints about your health register in your mind. Your psyche (mind) directs the energy in your body (soma) in the direction of your complaints.

"But I really am sick," you say. Please understand that I don't doubt that you believe you are. But remember that doctors estimate that 67 percent of illnesses are a result of "thinking sick." Our minds create our world, and our words indicate what we are thinking. Complaining about an illness will neither shorten its duration nor lessen its severity. In fact, it will often have the opposite effect.

> "The concept of total wellness recognizes that our every thought, word, and behavior affects our greater health and well-being. And we, in turn, are affected not only emotionally but also physically and spiritually."
>
> —GREG ANDERSON

I invite you to consider how often complaining about illness might be an unconscious attempt to get sympathy and attention or to avoid doing something. When you complain about your health, remember that you might be trying to put out a fire with gasoline. You might want to get healthy, but when you complain about your illness you are sending out health-limiting waves of energy throughout your body.

In 1999, a good friend of mine named Hal, who was

thirty-four at the time, was diagnosed with stage 4 lung cancer. The doctors gave him less than six months to live.

In addition to his terminal diagnosis, Hal was facing other challenges. Even though he had made his living selling health insurance, he had none. His bills piled up, and it was a constant struggle just to keep the lights on and his family fed. When I found out he was dying, I visited Hal and was astounded by his upbeat attitude. Hal didn't complain but talked about how great his life had been and how fortunate he was.

> "When any anxiety or gloom of the mind takes hold of you, make it a rule not to publish it by complaining; but exert yourselves to hide it, and by endeavoring to hide it you drive it away."
>
> —SAMUEL JOHNSON

Through it all, Hal kept his great sense of humor. One day I invited him to take a walk outdoors, but because he was so weak he managed only a dozen or so steps. We stood in front of his home savoring the fresh air and talked. As we did, Hal noticed several large buzzards making slow, lazy circles directly over where he stood. Hal pointed to the buzzards and said, "Oh, now, *that's* a bad sign!" When I saw the devilish glint in his eye, we both exploded into laughter.

When at last we caught our breath, I asked, "How do you manage to not complain with all you're going through?"

Hal leaned on his cane, smiled, and said, "'Easy, today isn't the fifteenth." Feeling he'd adequately answered my question, he turned and began to shuffle slowly back to the house.

"What the heck does today not being the fifteenth have to do with anything?" I asked, easily catching up to him.

Hal stopped and smiled, "When I was diagnosed, I knew it was going to be tough and that I could go through it cursing God, science, and everyone else. Or I could focus on the good things in my life. So I decided to give myself one unhappy day each month to complain. I randomly picked the fifteenth. Whenever anything happens that I might want to complain about, I tell myself that I have to wait until the fifteenth."

"Does that work?" I asked.

"Pretty well," he said.

"But don't you get really down on the fifteenth of each month?" I asked.

"Not really," he replied. "By the time the fifteenth gets here, I've usually forgotten what it was I was going to complain about."

Even though we lived more than two hours apart, I visited Hal twice a week until he made his life's transition. People would tell me what a great friend I was and how thoughtful I was to devote so much time to him. The truth is that I did it for me. Hal taught me that even in the midst of something as challenging as a terminal illness, we can find happiness.

Oh, and the doctors were wrong. Hal didn't die within six months of being diagnosed. He survived more than two happy years, feeling blessed and blessing those around him. Hal beat the medical experts' prediction by a factor of four. That's the health-affirming power of living a life of gratitude rather than one of complaint.

By this time in our journey, you've begun to get glimpses into what makes you gripe and how often you complain. You are becoming conscious of your incompetence.

PART 2

CONSCIOUS INCOMPETENCE

CHAPTER 3

COMPLAINING AND RELATIONSHIPS

He who avoids complaint invites happiness.

—ABU BAKR

Moving into the Conscious Incompetence stage means becoming uncomfortably aware of just how often you complain. You begin to catch yourself complaining but only after the fact, and you can't seem to stop. You repeatedly switch your bracelet, but your complaints don't seem to be diminishing. I've heard some refer to this as the "Stop me before I complain again" stage.

Sadly, many people give up at this point. For the first time, they are so conscious of how often they gripe, and their incompetence at restraining themselves is so uncomfortable, that they toss their bracelet in the drawer (or perhaps angrily out a window) and hope no one asks them about it.

If you're feeling uncomfortable right now, good! That

VOICES

I had reached a point in my career where I realized I had to improve my attitude on the job. One day at work, I phoned my wife and asked her to pick up some self-improvement books for me while she was at the library.

When I got home that evening, there were six books on the counter waiting for me. As I thumbed through each in turn, one book really caught my attention: A Complaint Free World, *by Will Bowen. I really liked the message it communicated. The stories were relatable, and I could not resist the challenge to go twenty-one days without complaining.*

I bought my own copy and began using a rubber band as my reminder. Several friends at work began to take the challenge. It became a game. We were texting each other asking what day we were on and sharing the encounters that had led us to reset our day count.

Soon sharing a cup of coffee became a task. We had to train ourselves to choose our words carefully to avoid complaining or gossiping.

The best change occurred for me at home. One night my wife and I were kissing in the kitchen, and she asked me, "Have you noticed we have been kissing more than usual?"

We discovered that I used to come home and complain about work, which would put us both in a bad

> *mood. This was not conducive to a loving relationship.*
> *My new approach of coming home and not complaining*
> *found us in a good mood and enjoying being together.*
>
> *It took me almost six months to get my first twenty-*
> *one days under my belt. I have changed the way I com-*
> *municate with others, and this has made me a happier*
> *person. I listen to the book on CD in my car frequently to*
> *keep myself on track.*
>
> —SHAWN O'CONNELL,
> ALBUQUERQUE, NEW MEXICO

discomfort means you're progressing. You're right on track, just stay with it. Remember the words of theologian Charles H. Spurgeon: "By perseverance the snail reached the ark." Regardless of how snail-like your progress seems, you are moving toward your ideal, and noticing your complaints, even if you can't yet stop them, is a step along the path.

I recently upgraded the operating system on the laptop computer I am using to write this book. I've had this computer for several years and like it very much. However, the standard configuration of the new operating system reversed the orientation of the computer's track pad. Previously, to scroll down the screen I swiped my

> "By perseverance the snail reached the ark."
>
> —CHARLES H. SPURGEON

finger in a downward motion on the track pad. However, most touch screens now employ the opposite movement to simulate the sensation of actually moving the screen with your fingers, and this is how the updated OS set my track pad.

What irony to be writing about the Conscious Incompetence stage when this happened. After more than two years, I had to move my fingers in the opposite direction to scroll up or down. For several days my fingers habitually moved one way while the screen image slid counter to where I wanted. My frustration was palpable and distracting. I *knew* that the track pad orientation had changed. I *knew* that I was doing it wrong. I kept telling myself to remember to move my finger in the opposite direction, but it was no use. After two years of doing it a certain way, I was not going to change immediately. It would take several uncomfortable days to retrain myself. I was hopelessly incompetent and very, very conscious of it.

It's been a week since I upgraded the operating system. My fingers now automatically slide in the new direction. I don't even have to think about it. In fact, it seems natural, as if it's the way I have always navigated documents. So if it feels like you're at the stage where you notice your complaints and want so very badly to quell them but can't, just relax and know that in time, you will retrain yourself.

Be patient. Great benefits await your making this change.

As we've discussed, complaining has caused you to focus on what is wrong, drawing your attention away from what you want. Complaining may also have limited your health. Complaining is also very damaging to relationships. In this chapter, we're going to review the highlights of how complaining can hinder or even destroy your relationships.

In 1938, Lewis Terman interviewed many psychiatrists and counselors in an attempt to identify a common thread in unhappy marriages. His research found that unhappy couples were distinguished from happy ones by the extent to which they reported their partner being argumentative, critical, and nagging (i.e., complaining). Further, in "A Descriptive Taxonomy of Couples' Complaint Interactions," Dr. J. K. Alberts reported, "Diverse research indicates that negativity and negative communication are positively correlated with relational dissatisfaction."

In other words, *unhappy relationships are most often distinguished by how much complaining occurs within the relationship.*

Complaining warps, weakens, and sometimes even destroys the very relationships that can bring us happiness. When we engage in complaining, our relationships stagnate and devolve. Complaining shifts our focus from the positive attributes that drew us to another person to what we perceive to be his or her faults. This shift draws us into a trap of feeling unfulfilled and can cause the other person to feel inadequate.

Complaining may bring social benefits such as attention and sympathy. Some people's relationships are based primarily on complaining, but a person who complains in such relationships walks a fine line. Studies have found that chronic complainers can end up ostracized even by others who complain, because their negative energy becomes excessively draining.

> The squeaky wheel may get the grease. But if it squeaks too much, it ends up getting replaced.

It's interesting that people tend to complain to friends, family members, and coworkers. However, most people want to *associate* with people who complain *less* than they do. We are drawn to people who are upbeat and who inspire us, even if those people are only slightly more positive than we are. So one way to dramatically improve your relationships with your spouse, friends, coworkers, and children is to begin to complain less.

Look at it from their point of view: given the chance, wouldn't you rather spend the day with Winnie-the-Pooh than with Eeyore?

You probably know people whose negativity leaves you feeling depleted. Comedian Dennis Miller once remarked, "There are people in this world who define themselves by their agitation." These people drain your energy. If an optimist views the glass as half full and a pessimist views it as half empty, a complainer will tell you that the water in the glass is probably poisoned.

Bestselling author and spiritual teacher Eckhart Tolle explains that everyone has what he calls a Pain Body. The Pain Body is that part of us that gets a rush from hearing bad news or from being in a confrontation with someone. Uncomfortable as these conditions may be, they are nonetheless stimulating, and some people are addicted to this negativity. It's like a drug they can't do without.

> "There are people in this world who define themselves by their agitation."
>
> —DENNIS MILLER

There is a term for this: pain addiction. When you experience pain, either real or imagined, your body squirts a shot of endorphins into your bloodstream. Endorphins are endogenous morphine, a powerful narcotic that is produced by your body's natural apothecary. This anesthetic is released when you experience pain, and complaining ignites emotional pain.

It goes like this: complaining triggers pain, pain triggers endorphins, and endorphins get you high. You probably don't notice this elevated state any more than a heavy coffee drinker notices a caffeine rush, but just as the coffee drinker trying to kick caffeine will experience withdrawal, so, too, will the person giving up complaining.

With regards to relationships, remember that both you and the other person have a proclivity to activate your pain body to produce a shot of endorphins. This understanding alone can help you regain your sanity in the midst of an uncomfortable exchange.

The common factor in unhappy relationships is that one or both people complain to or about the other person. Complaining is draining and unfulfilling, and it makes you feel agitated and even defensive.

As you become Complaint Free, don't expect other people to silence their complaints immediately. Again, to look at complaining as a drug, many of us have been in situations where others were drinking excessively, smoking, or doing drugs. If someone does not go along with the group, the individuals in the group feel threatened. My personal theory regarding this phenomenon is that people engaging in destructive behaviors know that they are not acting in their best interest, and this knowledge is magnified in the presence of someone who is not partaking.

> "Like attracts like."
>
> —RICHARD BACH,
> *ILLUSIONS*

When we're around others who complain more or less than we do, it feels uncomfortable. Our vibration levels are different and people of different energy repel one another.

In his book *Illusions* Richard Bach wrote a simple and profound truth: "Like attracts like." People who are alike, be they pessimists or optimists, attract those of similar energy. We are all energy beings, and energy that does not vibrate at the same frequency does not harmonize. Like attracts like.

It's sad but true that rather than others supporting you in your efforts to become Complaint Free, many people will attempt to discourage you and to dissuade you from this positive transformation.

In 1967 a study was done with rhesus monkeys that reflects this tendency in humans. A single toy was placed in a cage of rhesus monkeys, and whenever one of them approached the toy, that monkey was punished (exactly how it was punished is not disclosed).

When a new monkey, one that had not been punished for pursuing the toy, was placed in the cage, the other monkeys attacked it whenever it went for the toy. The monkeys not participating in the attack jumped about arching their backs and acting aggressively.

Friends, family, coworkers, even acquaintances are threatened when we try and break out of the pack, when we go for a toy such as a better life. Although you are attempting to do something in your best interest, many will attempt to thwart your efforts. Ironically, once you have become a happier person these same individuals will come to you wanting to know your secret. At this point, just smile and hand them a purple bracelet.

One of the great myths about complaining is that people

feel that they must complain to get others to change. You have never complained anyone, including yourself, into positive change. Rather, when you complain to someone, you define that person as one who engages in the behavior you are complaining about, and they are more, not less, likely to repeat it.

When you say, "You always leave your socks on the floor," the other person will continue to drop his or her socks on the floor. It's like a *Star Wars* Jedi mind trick. Your comment registers in the other person's psyche, defining him or her as someone who deposits dirty socks on the floor, and that perpetuates the behavior. It is far better to ask the other person for what you want and then praise him or her (without sarcasm) when the person begins to act even remotely as you would like.

> You have never complained anyone, including yourself, into positive change.

I know of a group of women here in Kansas City that gathers each week for what they call "Group Therapy." They meet at a Mexican restaurant to drink margaritas and complain about men. From what I am told, their underlying theme is "All men are dogs!"

Well, if you've just spent several hours complaining to your friends that the man in your life is a dog, it's not surprising that you see Old Yeller sitting in the La-Z-Boy when you get home. Your mind looks for validation for what you have been saying. Your complaints become an unpleasant self-fulfilling prophecy.

Not one of these Group Therapy women is in a happy and fulfilling relationship with a man. Do they want such a relationship? Sure, but through their complaints, they are sending out energetic vibrations that "men are dogs," causing them to look for and attract men that display doglike behavior.

Seek and ye shall find. They are creating their reality with their complaints.

Now, you might feel that they are in relationships with unloving men and are just gathering with others in similarly problematic relationships to share their truth and garner support. But consider that their complaining is perpetuating their unhappiness by defining their relationships as problematic.

Your words indicate, reinforce, and perpetuate your thoughts. So when you complain, you are actually repelling what you profess to want. Griping pushes away from you things that you say you would like to have.

A couple I'll call Rowland and Lorraine met another couple that had a young son who was about the same age as their daughter. The adults had a lot in common and the kids loved playing with each other, so the families began to spend a lot of time together. Over the course of several months, both Rowland and Lorraine found that they began to dread these get-togethers.

One night Lorraine said, "I really like those two, but whenever she and I are alone all she does is complain about her husband."

"He does the same thing," said Rowland. "He gripes constantly about her, too. Not only that, he also seems intent on ferreting out any problems that we might be having."

Misery not only loves company, it derives validation from it. Over time, Rowland and Lorraine excused themselves from spending time with the other couple and ultimately severed all contact with them.

Becoming Complaint Free means beginning to practice healthy communication skills. It is not complaining to speak directly and only to the person who can resolve an issue. Rather than complaining to Rowland and Lorraine, this couple should have been talking to each other to work through their challenges.

It is not complaining to speak directly and only to the person who can resolve an issue.

This seems obvious, but it is not the norm for most people. When most people are unhappy with their boss, they complain to their spouse. When they are displeased with their spouse, they complain to their friends. They speak to anyone and everyone except the person who can actually improve the situation, and they live in disappointment and bewilderment, wondering why their relationships don't improve.

Relationships serve two purposes:

1. Fun
2. Growth

The fun is the pleasure we derive from our association with the other person. The growth comes from the relationship calling up unhealed issues. When we are with someone for a prolonged period of time, old stuff will come up. There's a line in the song "Don't Worry 'Bout a Thing" by the band Shedaisy, "We've all got a little junk in the trunk," and relationships open up our trunks so we can deal with the junk.

Rather than dealing with issues by talking them out with the person involved, most people blame the other person and complain to friends to validate their being a victim. In reality, the relationship is placing the issue squarely before their eyes so they can work through it once and for all.

Talking to someone other than the person with whom you have a problem is triangulation. Triangulation occurs when you experience a challenge with someone but discuss the situation with someone else. Healthy communication is speaking directly and only to the person with whom you have an issue.

> "It is impossible to suffer without making someone pay for it; every complaint already contains revenge."
>
> —FRIEDRICH NIETZSCHE

Triangulation is complaining, and it perpetuates rather than solves problems.

You may have experienced this in your own life. One of your children may be upset with a sibling but come to you instead. You, the wise parent, get involved by either advising the discontented child what to do, or worse, talking to the other child yourself. In the short term, you may resolve the current situation, but you are not providing your children with the tools they need to resolve future issues. You are allowing the complaining child to remain a victim in the situation and are establishing a pattern of triangulation for future challenges.

Certainly you want to help and support your children, but when you try and resolve their issues with one another, you are not modeling healthy communication. Further, you are unconsciously inviting your children to involve you regularly in future conflicts, regardless of their scale or importance.

Consider inviting them to talk to one another instead, trusting their own internal guidance to resolve their conflicts. In so doing, you are giving them the gift of healthy communication. More important, you are helping them to realize that they have the power to improve challenging situations.

Triangulation is rampant in many churches. I recently heard of one minister talking to another about the way a third minister was leading his church. After several minutes of listening to the first minister's criticisms, the listener—who had remained silent up until that point—pressed the speaker button on his phone and called the minister being vilified.

When the third minister answered the phone, the second minister said, "Ed? This is Jerry. I've got you on speakerphone and I'm sitting here with Mike. Mike was just sharing some feelings he has about how you lead your church. I don't want to be a partner to triangulation, and I know you'd value the feedback he's so willing to share. So, Ed, here's Mike."

Reverend Mike sat in stunned silence, his face blazing. Finally he mumbled a few comments and reached past Jerry to disconnect the call. Then he stood and walked swiftly out of Jerry's office.

In that moment, Reverend Mike clearly got the message that triangulation is out of integrity, and Jerry drew a healthy boundary, assuring that he would no longer have to listen to Mike's criticisms of a fellow minister.

Here's a bit of sobering news: You wouldn't notice the faults in someone else if they were not also your faults. People who order Complaint Free purple bracelets for "all the whiny people around them" tend to discover when they arrive that they themselves are profuse complainers. If you are honest with yourself, you will find that the things that upset you about others are traits

> "If we had no faults of our own, we would not take so much pleasure in noticing those of others."
>
> —FRANÇOIS DE LA ROCHEFOUCAULD

you share with them. You're just in the unconscious incompetent stage regarding that part of your personality, and relationships with others serve to make you conscious of it.

If you feel compelled to point out something negative about someone else, do some digging first to see if you share the trait, and be grateful for this chance to now be aware of it so you can work on it. As you discover and begin to integrate these fragmented parts of your personality—that is, begin to love and accept your quirks—those same quirks in others will cease to disturb you.

And, please don't let the other side of this truth escape you. The things you admire in others appeal to you for the same reason—they are aspects you share. What you admire about another person is also within you. Those positive traits may lie dormant for now, but if you focus on them and look for them, they will bubble forth from within you.

People in relationships entrain with each other. You create your reality through your thoughts and words, and this energy vibrates out to others. Each person's energy contributes to the course of a relationship. Like a great river, the relationship twists and turns, and the people in it are caught up in its flow. People shift in relationships even when they are unaware they are doing so.

Here's a simple way to see how relationships influence people and how the people in them will tend to meld toward being like each other. The next time you are part of an audience that begins to applaud, notice that if the clapping continues long enough the audience will begin to clap at the same time. The clapping will establish a rhythm. This is called entrainment. People in relationships entrain with each other.

I've demonstrated this many times when speaking to large crowds, instructing the audience to clap and continue clapping until I ask them to stop. It may take only seconds, or at other times it takes a minute or two, but it always happens. The applause falls into a beat, a cadence; this group of individuals begins to clap as if they were synchronized human metronomes—they entrain.

Entrainment is a principle just as gravity is a principle and is therefore neither good nor bad—it simply is. And, just like gravity, it's always working. You are constantly synching up with those around you. You are entraining with them and they are entraining with you. When you are around others who complain, you will find yourself tending to complain more often. And when you begin to complain less frequently, those about you will complain less.

To improve your relationships, don't wait for others to stop complaining. Commit to being the positive force in the relationship. The change you seek is never "out there," it is within. St. Francis of Assisi put it this way: "What you are looking for is what is looking."

"What you are looking for is what is looking."

—ST. FRANCIS OF ASSISI

To improve your relationships, continue to improve yourself. Who you are and what you say impacts and directs all of your relationships.

Whenever two people get together, the resulting conversation is an organic, evolving entity. It meanders from topic to topic directed by the comments of those assembled. The discussion of a group of people can be likened to the movement of a flock of birds.

Have you ever noticed a large flock of birds gliding in slow, shifting waves across a dull gray sky? Seemingly as one living being, the flock may flow gently one way, hover momentarily, and then shift lazily back. Then, as if on cue, the birds dart suddenly upward, forming a tight spiral, before spilling down to land en masse in an empty field.

Scientists who have studied the ballet-like choreography of birds theorized that there must be an individual leader guiding the movements of the flock. The researchers sought to identify subtle cues coming from a lead bird that directed the group, but they couldn't discern a leader. Each bird's actions define the movement of the flock. As a bird decides whether to go left or right, speed up or slow down, climb higher or dip lower, the surrounding birds react and the flock moves accordingly. Every single bird determines the shape, movement, speed, altitude, and direction of the flock. The kaleidoscopic inkblot we see as a flock is actually thousands of individual decisions made moment by moment.

Conversations are similarly free formed and group led. Someone may mention a book and the discussion will flutter toward books for a time. If the book mentioned is about camping, the conversation may meander over to the subject of camping. A conversation is a great symphony where a melody is played until there is a subtle shift by one of the instruments, causing a whole new tune to unfold that carries the orchestra along.

In conversations, complaining tends to evolve subtly and insidiously. Just as a slight movement by a single bird sends a ripple throughout the flock, a single complaint can spread all the way through a gathering of people, dragging down the tone and mood of the whole.

It happens innocently enough. One person will complain and, in so doing, receive attention and/or sympathy from the group. Without even realizing his motivation is to receive similar interest, another person will complain but make his grievance sound worse when compared to the first. You can almost hear the collective "Ahhhh . . ." as the attention of the group shifts to the second complainer. Not to be outdone, the first complainer will often embellish the original complaint, or possibly, a third person will chime in attempting to out-complain the first two. Soon an all-out competition ensues.

Notice that complaining in groups always progresses in severity. The next time you're with a group of people, notice what generally happens when someone complains. Another person will then tell a story that is on the same topic but contains an even more terrible outcome. Someone else will attempt to outdo the first two, and soon the whole group is scouring their minds hoping to share their most catastrophic experience involving the subject before the group. The flock, which may have been ascending toward a glimmering sunrise, now begins to dive down into a black ravine.

Complaining is a competitive sport. It is always progressive. If someone complains about having sprained an ankle while skiing, another person will tell a story about breaking a leg. The first person may then complain to the group that a sprain hurts considerably more and takes longer to heal than a break. The second person will state that although some sprains are worse than breaks, it was not so in this case, and to emphasize the point he or she will pull up a pant leg to reveal a scar where pins and screws were inserted to surgically repair the broken bone.

Complaining is a competitive sport.

Complaints always run in one direction—toward a more

dire experience. Imagine sitting around with friends when someone complains about losing his job and his girlfriend in the same week. Then someone else laments having suffered through a painful hangnail and a pimple all in a seven-day period. The group would look at the second complainer as if she were insane. Complaining in groups always increases in severity.

A great example of the one-upmanship element of complaining was presented by the British comedy troupe Monty Python's Flying Circus in their skit "The Four Yorkshiremen," which was released on their 1974 album *Live at Drury Lane*.

In the sketch, four sophisticated and well-dressed gentlemen from Yorkshire, England, are seated together enjoying some expensive wine. Their conversation begins with statements of shared gratitude for their successes, shifts subtly negative, and then, over time, the complaining one-upmanship becomes excessive to the point of hilarity.

One gentleman comments that, in previous years, he would have been lucky to afford the price of a cup of tea. A second, wanting to outdo the first, says that he would have been fortunate to have purchased *cold* tea.

The others join in and the complaining revs up. Soon their comments spiral into ludicrousness as each tries to prove that his life was the one of greatest hardship. One of the gentlemen tells of the shabby condition of the house he lived in as a boy. The second clicks his tongue, rolls his eyes, and replies, "House! You were lucky to live in a house! We used to live in one room, all twenty-six of us, no furniture, half the floor was missing, and we were all huddled together in one corner for fear of falling."

Back and forth the lamentations continue, growing more dismal each time, as another says, "Eh, you were lucky to have a room! We used to have to live in the corridor!"

"Oh, we used to dream of living in a corridor!" says another. "We used to live in an old water tank on a rubbish tip. We got woke up every morning by having a load of rotting fish dumped all over us!"

"Well, when I say 'house' it was only a hole in the ground covered by a sheet of tarpaulin, but it was a house to us."

"We were evicted from our 'ole in the ground; we had to go and live in a lake."

"You were lucky to have a lake! There were a hundred and fifty of us living in a shoe box in the middle of road."

Finally, one of the gentlemen decides the competition has gone far enough. With a determined look in his eyes he says, "All right then." Taking a deep breath and sitting up straight, he says, "I had to get up in the morning at ten o'clock at night half an hour before I went to bed, drink a cup of sulfuric acid, work twenty-nine hours a day down in a mill, and pay the mill owner for permission to come to work. And when we got home, our dad and our mother would kill us and dance about on our graves singing, 'Hallelujah!'"

Becoming a Complaint Free person means that you shift your emotional compass from negative to positive. However, you are and will be surrounded by others who are complaining to and about you. Their negativity can entice you to join in and to carry the complaining baton on to someone else.

I walked into a local restaurant the other day, and as the hostess led me to my table I overheard a man humming "Here Comes the Sun" by the Beatles. The restaurant was a buffet, and as I was in line serving myself, I found that I was now humming the same tune.

After I finished my lunch, I walked to a nearby store and saw a woman shopping there who had been standing next to me in the restaurant buffet line. She was now humming "Here Comes the Sun," presumably because she had heard me humming the song. I fell to wondering who might hear her and begin to hum the same tune and who might then hear that person and how far it might travel.

Our words, be they upbeat or negative, spread to others in just the same fashion. We can choose to add to the world's negativity by spreading complaints or we can resolve to let the complaining stop with us.

I received a call from a minister in Louisiana informing me that the "Complaint Free idea was a bust!"

"How so?" I asked.

"I gave the bracelets out in my church, and I did a series of talks on the idea, but my congregation complains as much now as ever."

"How long did it take you to complete the twenty-one days?" I asked.

"I didn't," she said. "I've been having a tough time, so I set the bracelet aside."

I reminded her of a quote from the great Roman philosopher Publilius Syrus, "Anyone can hold the helm when the sea is calm," and suggested she put her bracelet on and begin to lead by example. She muttered something and quickly hung up. I've not heard from her since.

Somehow she had missed the core concept of leadership and a key to positive relationships. We must set an example for others to follow. Benjamin Franklin put it this way: "The best sermon is a good example." And Gandhi said, "We must live what we want others to learn." If you want others to change and your relationships to improve, you must change first.

> "We must live what we want others to learn."
>
> —GANDHI

As I mentioned, thanks to the explosion of the Complaint Free concept, I have been fortunate to speak to groups and corporations around the world. The organizations where the leaders took the challenge themselves and worked at completing the twenty-one days saw great improvements in morale and business. Their employees were eager to join in, and the whole experience built a positive framework and sense of community.

However, the organizations that brought in the "Complaint Free guy" in hopes of shutting up their malcontented employees and/or customers saw little if any benefit.

When bosses, parents, ministers, coaches, or family leaders order the purple bracelets wanting to "get everyone around me to stop complaining," I find myself wanting to include a little note: "Warning, this will not work unless you do."

The Complaint Free idea would have gone nowhere had I not gone through the laborious process of changing my own bracelet thousands of times until I reached twenty-one consecutive Complaint Free days and had I not reported honestly all the while how I was progressing.

Do you want your friends, children, parents, spouse, brother, sister, boss, fellow employees, and others to lay off the griping? Someone must lead the flock. Someone must dare to go his or her own direction, even if it means bumping into the adjacent birds from time to time.

If you are a leader and want those in your charge to become more upbeat, then remember that a leader is out front, facing the frontier and blazing the trail for others to follow.

If you find yourself in a nest of complainers, consider that you probably belong in that nest. As you are discovering in your sojourn to become Complaint Free, you complain a lot more than you thought, and like attracts like.

When I was striving to go twenty-one consecutive days without complaining, I found that after a month or so I could string together several days in a row without complaining. Then, I would get a call from my friend Scott (not his real name).

After one conversation during which I switched my bracelet four times, I told a mutual friend, "I'm going to have to avoid Scott until I make the twenty-one days. His negativity is so contagious I fall into complaining whenever we speak."

"I've never noticed him to be negative," she said.

"You haven't?" I asked.

"No," she said. "Here's usually cheerful and offers optimistic observations about what's going on in his life and mine, too."

> "We have met the enemy and he is us."
>
> —POGO

That took a moment to sink in. Perhaps *my* default mode of communication with Scott was complaining. The next time he called, I resolved to sit in absolute silence if need be rather than complain. I didn't complain and, surprisingly, neither did he.

Pogo was right: "We have met the enemy and he is us."

When I stopped complaining to Scott, the conversation ceased to be a fertile ground for negativity.

Countless people have told me that as they strove to become Complaint Free, complaining people were simply no longer attracted to them. Therefore, the best way to get others around you to complain less is for you to become a Complaint Free person. Others will sense your positive energy and be less likely to offer negativity.

The first step toward all positive change is acceptance of a person's current state. Pushing someone to change only causes that person to cling more doggedly to his or her current mode of being.

Recently, Japan was struck by one of the worst earthquakes in that nation's history. Several years ago, an earthquake rocked China.

The Japanese and Chinese use the same symbol to describe a building designed to withstand an earthquake. However, in Japanese the symbol is translated as "tolerate" or "accept"; in Chinese the symbol is translated as "fight." Therefore, in Japanese, a building built to withstand an earthquake is said to "tolerate" the earthquake, whereas the same building in Chinese is said to "fight" the earthquake.

Earthquakes send out ripples from their epicenters, impacting everything they touch. Complaints radiate outward and impact everyone who hears them. I mentioned previously that because you are reading this book you now notice complaints and complainers like never before. You may also find yourself experiencing negative and resentful feelings toward rampant complainers. When this happens, consider the differences in the Japanese and Chinese translations of the same symbol.

If your intention is to fight complainers, you will have a much more difficult time than if you first tolerate and accept them.

CHAPTER 4

WHY WE COMPLAIN

Negativity can only feed on negativity.

–ELISABETH KÜBLER-ROSS

D r. Robin Kowalski of Clemson University identified five reasons that people complain. As you hear yourself and others complain, you will find that all complaints are spoken for one or more of these reasons.

Here's a mnemonic device that I created to help remember the five reasons people complain; the acronym is G.R.I.P.E.:

Get attention
Remove responsibility
Inspire envy
Power
Excuse poor performance

VOICES

I first learned of this wonderful program on the Today *show. I began asking my coworkers if they would be interested in doing this. The majority of them agreed and we ordered our bracelets. We decided that while we were waiting for them to arrive, we would set one day of our business week aside and try not to complain on that given day. We now set Mondays aside as NO MOAN MONDAYS.*

We have signs posted on our company bulletin board and around the office to remind employees to try not to moan, gripe, or complain on Mondays. It really has been an inspiration in our office and we usually greet each other on Mondays with "Welcome to No Moan Monday!"

When you think about it, life is just too short. We are always looking for those big blessings in life (e.g., more money, job security, weight loss, etc.), but we need to start looking for those tiny blessings that are given to us each day.

I think this program is wonderful. We are so blessed!

—SALLY SCUDIERE,

KENT, OHIO

Get attention Human beings have an innate need to be acknowledged by other people. Attention from others makes them feel safe, secure, and cared for. Being recognized by others makes them feel that they belong, that they are part of the tribe. People will often complain simply because they want attention from others and can't think of another, more positive means of getting the notice they crave.

The weather, work, their intimate partner, their children, the economy, and local sports teams are favorite topics of people complaining to get your attention. What this type of complainer is really saying is "Hey, notice me! I want to talk to you. I want to get your attention, and I'm completely lost as to what to say other than to gripe about something."

If there is someone at work who tends to come into your workspace frequently to complain, consider that that person might just want attention. Then take direct action by going to him or her first to ask a question. Ask about the person's hobbies, family, health, etc. Give attention to this person first so he or she doesn't feel the need to come and solicit it through complaining.

You might think, "I don't have time for that." Well, do you have time for your coworker continually coming to you with complaints? Are you committed to changing your association with this person?

Here's a great technique to get the conversation off on a

positive note. Ask, "So, what's going well with . . . [you, your family, your work, your hobby, etc.]?"

The compulsive complainer will probably respond by telling you what is *not* going well with regards to whatever topic you threw out. This person is so accustomed to griping to get attention that it never occurs to him or her that it's possible to have a positive connection with someone. Rather than fighting this response, accept it. Consider this to be like training a parrot to speak. It will take patience and repeated effort, but it's worth it to establish a new foundation with the person.

When your coworker starts to complain, smile and delicately interrupt, asking again, "Yes, but what is going *well* with . . ." Or "Yes, but what do you *like* about . . ." Or "Yes, but how would you *ideally* like to see this working out?"

> When someone complains to **Get attention**, ask, "What is going well for you?"

Just as it can take many weeks of switching your bracelet to complete one full Complaint Free day, it may take quite a few redirections to get your coworker to even consider that there are indeed some good aspects to his or her life. Be patient and have compassion. Remember that this type of complainer lives in fear that not griping will mean not being able to connect with other people.

Be persistent, and one of two things will occur: The

complainer will either begin to complain less to you or begin to avoid you.

That's right, your gentle insistence that your interactions be positive, as evidenced by your redirecting questions, will either modify your coworker's behavior or cause him or her to stay away from you.

Just as you may have dreaded seeing this person come your way in the past, when you are diligent in soliciting a positive response, your coworker may begin to equally dread being around you. A person who is totally immersed in the Pain Body, with no desire to emerge, is every bit as repelled by your upbeat questions as you are by his or her complaints.

Either way, you win.

Remove responsibility This complainer says, "What do you want from me?" "It's impossible." "You can't fight city hall." "It's Marketing's fault." "The dog ate my homework." "She was supposed to wake me up." "The traffic was terrible." "No one will help me." And more—much, much more.

This type of complainer seeks to build a case for his or her inability to achieve by painting a hopeless picture as to the outcome. "There's no use," the complainer is saying. "So I'm not going to try." And this complainer is soliciting agreement from those who hear his or her complaints so as to validate that victimhood.

These complainers seek to blame other people and circumstances to justify their own lack of effort. They blame their parents, the economy, their lack of education, their age, and anything that may seem plausible. They are consumed with blame.

"Responsibility: A detachable burden easily shifted to the shoulders of God, Fate, Fortune, Luck or one's neighbor. In the days of astrology it was customary to unload it upon a star."

—AMBROSE BIERCE

In his book *The Presence Process*, Michael Brown accurately breaks down the word "blame" as to "be lame." A person who complains to blame the world and other people for his or her life is being lame; that person feels powerless to make things better. This type of person will reject any suggestion you offer as to how things might be improved. He or she does not want your suggestions, but rather your concurrence that he or she is an impotent, helpless victim.

It goes like this: The person complains to you about a problem, so you proffer a possible solution. The suggestion is immediately shot down with another complaint as to how it won't work. Again, you put forth something the person might try, and this, too, is discounted. In his book *Games People Play*, Eric Berne refers to this as the "Why Don't You . . . Yes But" game. You suggest a solution, "Why don't you . . . ," and the person's immediate response is "Yes but . . . ," and he or she then proceeds to tell you all the reasons why your suggestion will not work.

People seeking to "be lame" can play this game for hours. They are not looking for you to help discover ways to accomplish a task or solve a problem. Based on their comments you might think so, but they're not. They are trying to get you to admit that the problem is irresolvable. They have constructed a case for why it cannot be done, and if you agree to their reasons, it justifies their inaction. They want to be removed from the responsibility of creating a solution and want you to validate this position.

Super-motivator Tony Robbins has a brilliant way of handling such people. I learned it at one of his seminars more than twenty years ago and have used it thousands of times, and it surprises me each time how well it has works. When a person says, "It can't be done," your response should be "If it *was* possible, how might you do it?"

> When someone complains to **Remove responsibility,** ask, "If it *was* possible, how might you do it?"

When you read this, it may sound dismissive or so obviously manipulative that you wonder if the complaining person will accuse you of trying to trick him or her. However, as I said, it works! As someone begins to pile on all the reasons why something can't be done, keep asking, "If it was possible, how might you do it?" This can open the complainer's mind to considering possibilities where once that person saw only limitations. He or she will begin to think of ways of accomplishing the task and shift focus to making it happen.

If asking, "If this was possible, how might you do it?" does not shift the person away from his or her "Yes, buts," simply say, "I have faith in your ability to figure out a way to accomplish this." Then, with every complaining justification as to how impossible the task is, simply repeat, "I have faith in your ability to figure out a way to accomplish this."

This works particularly well with children.

As with the previous suggestion about getting someone to stop complaining to get attention, the person complaining to remove him or herself from responsibility may write you off as a crank and simply keep a safe distance from you. Again, either way you win, because that person will cease to trot out complaints to you.

Inspire envy People often complain to inspire envy; that is: to brag. A person will complain about someone else as a means of saying that he or she does not have the perceived character flaw being complained about.

"My boss is so stupid" is a backhanded way of saying "I'm

smarter than my boss, and if I was in charge, things would be better." "My husband is a slob" is the complainer bragging that she is neat. "She drives like a maniac" translates to "I am a safe and courteous driver."

This is unconscious on the part of the complainer. And your task is to help that person shift away from this need to magnify himself or herself with negative comparisons. People complaining to inspire envy are actually trying to get you to appreciate them. They feel empty and attack someone else as a means of making themselves look better.

Gossip is complaining to inspire envy. When you gossip, you should switch your bracelet. The underlying message behind gossip is that the gossip feels superior to the person being gossiped about and wants you to acknowledge this.

> "No one gossips about other people's secret virtues."
>
> —BERTRAND RUSSELL

Gossip is speaking negatively about someone who is not present. I'm not saying you can't talk about other people. What I'm suggesting is that you:

1. Talk only about the positive traits of those who are absent
2. Say the same things and with the same inflection that you would say if the person was present

"But that takes all the fun out of it," many have said to me.

Exactly. Gossips are not speaking to share information; they are pointing out what they perceive to be another's negative traits so as to appear superior by comparison.

In the movie *Hitch*, Kevin James's character is dating a wealthy young woman who invites him to a party with her socialite friends. Two of her acquaintances approach, and she starts a conversation asking if either of them has seen an art exhibit that just opened.

"It's disgusting," says one.

Attempting to keep the discussion upbeat, the young woman asks, "Have you tried the new restaurant in Midtown?"

"Disgusting!" says the other of her acquaintances dismissively.

These two young men were not trying to share their opinions of either the art gallery exhibit or the restaurant. They were saying, "We are so refined that nothing measures up to our high standards."

> When someone complains to **Inspire envy**, compliment that person for possessing the opposite trait.

The way to shift this type of complainer is really quite simple. When someone begins to complain about a negative attribute that person perceives another person to possess, compliment the complainer on *hav-*

ing the opposite trait. If, for example, someone says, "He gets angry at the least little thing," your response might be "One of the things I admire about you is your ability to stay calm in difficult situations."

"She dresses like a homeless person," someone might complain.

"You always dress so well. I'm proud to be seen with you," you say.

"She is backbiting and mean," the complainer may gripe.

"You always treat people so well. Have I told you how much I appreciate that about you?" you affirm.

People complaining or gossiping to inspire envy are trying to get you to agree with them. If you do, you are only inviting further complaints. Instead, take the focus off the person being complained about and put it where the complainer wishes it to be, on him or her! Strive to have the presence of mind to compliment the complainer for being the opposite of what that person is complaining about.

Don't explain why you are doing this; to do so would negate the power of this technique. Instead, listen for the core idea behind the complaint and compliment the complainer for being the polar opposite.

This will stop the complaints immediately, as you rest in a moment of the complainer's stunned silence. The complainer will probably start in again about the other person. Again, you compliment the complainer. Soon that person will feel emotionally full and have no more need to complain.

Power Complaints are often the currency with which one purchases power.

Power is authority.

Power is privilege.

Power is ease.

Power is salve on a bruised and hurting ego.

The quest to acquire and maintain power is the driving force in many people's lives. They attempt to mask the internal void within their souls with an external attempt to control others.

> "Being powerful is like being a lady. If you have to tell people you are, you aren't."
>
> —MARGARET THATCHER

When something happens, you can let it pass, work it out, or go to war. Complaining is often recruiting soldiers to fight on your side.

Complaining can be a means of building support against a rival should a power struggle arise. You will see people complaining to garner power in corporations, churches, families, civic groups, homeowners' associations—anywhere and everywhere people gather into groups. One person covets a position of authority and complains about his or her competitors in order to purchase other people's loyalty.

A person complaining for power is saying, "If it ever comes down to me against him, here are the reasons you should be on my side."

I flew to Washington, DC, to speak, and when I arrived, I went outside the airport to catch a shuttle to my hotel. The driver placed my bags in the back and held the van door open for me to enter. There was only one seat left, and as I slid into it I noticed the man sitting next to me. His clothing concerned me.

It was a hot day in DC, nearly ninety degrees, and yet my seatmate wore a heavy three-quarter-length wool coat, gloves that went all the way to his elbows, and not one but two ski masks. I had just left the airport having been told that the terrorist threat level was at orange, and now here I was seated next to a terrorist poster child.

And to make matters worse, the man leaned over to repeatedly ask me, "What time is it?"

"It's time to get the heck out of this van," I thought to myself.

In time it came to light that he was an author and was running late for a radio interview. I shared with him that I, too, am an author and asked about the book he was promoting.

He said he worked for one of the two major U.S. political parties and his job was to dig up everything negative or anything that could take a negative spin about the other party's presidential candidate. His research would be used by his candidate's campaign team to prepare negative ads to sway voters.

"I've written a how-to book on dirty campaigning," he said.

He then asked, "So, what are your books about?" I stifled a laugh as I told him that my books were about the power of *not* complaining. A prolonged and uncomfortable silence followed.

Wanting to change the subject I asked, "It's really warm today. Why are you dressed in such heavy clothes?"

"It's the strangest thing," he said. "I used to live here in Washington, but I now have to live in Florida. When I'm here, I'm prone to convulsive, gasping asthma attacks. I have to dress this way or else I'll react to something in the air in DC and won't be able to breathe."

As we pulled up to his hotel I thought to myself, "How interesting . . . your job is to foul the airwaves and you can't breathe. Buddy, you make your own lunch."

I never did get the man's name. I don't know how well his book fared. I do know that negative advertising is used frequently in political campaigns because it works. Elections are not won by getting enough people to vote for a candidate; they are won by getting enough people so disgusted that they either do not vote or vote for the opposing candidate. Complaining is a very effective means of garnering power.

When a child complains to you about a sibling, a person at work complains about a boss or fellow employee, a member of your homeowners' association complains about another member, or others complain to you in an attempt to sway you to support their position, the best thing to do is to invite that person to go and speak directly to the person being complained about.

"But I have," the person will probably say, "and it hasn't done any good."

"Then it sounds like the two of you have more to talk about," you say. Step aside and don't get involved.

> When someone complains to you about someone else in order to gain **Power**, invite that person to speak directly to the person being complained about.

When two gorillas are fighting, it's best to stay out of the jungle.

Refuse to take sides. A person complaining to purchase your loyalty will cease when he or she realizes that your loyalty is not for sale.

Excuse poor performance Unlike the person complaining to justify inaction, a person complaining to excuse his or her poor performance complains about circumstances *after* the fact to explain away failure.

"The sun was in my eyes."
"He bumped me just as I took the shot."

"I need a new grip on this stupid golf club."

"You didn't wake me in time."

Complaining to excuse poor performance is an attempt to rationalize (tell yourself rational lies) by saying circumstances were stacked against you.

"It's not my fault" is the underlying message of such a complainer.

Like the other types of complaining, this one works. People gain justification for their having fallen short of optimal performance.

On July 6, 1993, the Thomas & Mack Center in Las Vegas, Nevada, shook with excitement. George Foreman was getting a shot at the World Boxing Organization's heavyweight title at the age of forty-four, an age considered well past the prime for any boxer. This appeared to be Foreman's one final and desperate attempt to regain a heavyweight title. That night, Foreman was to fight rising star Tommy "The Duke" Morrison, who was twenty years his junior. It had been nearly two decades since Foreman had held a major title.

Foreman, who was infamous for his temper and sullen attitude as a young man, was now returning to the sport a humble, upbeat, and righteous man.

The fight lasted the full twelve rounds, with Foreman refusing to sit in his corner between bouts. Later he would explain, "At my age I was afraid that if I sat down I'd never be able to get up again."

Foreman's strength and reach were legendary, and although Morrison was a well-trained powerhouse, he refused to stand toe-to-toe with Foreman. Round after round Morrison danced and retreated. Feeling cheated, the spectators booed Morrison.

Foreman was able to land some significant punches when he could catch The Duke, but Morrison countered well. As the eleventh round came to a close, the HBO commentators stated that Foreman was probably behind on points and needed a decisive twelfth round to win.

> "If you say something is not possible, what you are really saying is, 'I don't want it.'"
>
> —SADHGURU JAGGI

As the television cameras drew in tight on the sweating and panting Foreman standing shakily in his corner, his fight team told him that they were sure he was *ahead* on points and that Foreman could coast the last round and still win. His team was not seeing what the commentators and fans could see: that although Foreman had fought well, Morrison was, in fact, ahead.

Foreman took the advice of his team and backed off for round 12.

Foreman lost.

When the unanimous decision was announced, reporters pounced on Foreman, asking how he felt having been given bad advice from his crew. Wasn't he angry? Didn't he feel cheated?

Foreman ignored their questions. Foreman didn't complain. He made no mention of the advice he had received. With a sincere smile, he congratulated Morrison and thanked those who had helped and supported him, including the crew in his corner.

Had George Foreman blown his only chance at a comeback? Not by a long shot. Even though he was now unranked as a fighter and undeserving of another opportunity, he was nonetheless afforded another chance, and in 1994 Foreman won both the World Boxing Association *and* the International Boxing Federation heavyweight titles. He then went on to become one of the great product pitchmen of the latter part of twentieth century, as well as enjoying success as a sports commentator.

> "That's my gift. I let that negativity roll off me like water off a duck's back. If it's not positive, I didn't hear it. If you can overcome that, fights are easy."
>
> —GEORGE FOREMAN

Some say it was Foreman's unyielding tenacity that brought him success in the second chapter of his life. Indeed, when he began to train for a comeback, Foreman would have his wife drive him ten miles away from their home in a suburb of Houston, Texas, and drop him off on the side of the road. Foreman said that this was the only way he could force himself to run that far.

Others say Foreman's phoenix-like rise to newfound fame and fortune on the backside of forty was attributable to his connection with God. From the gloomy, discordant man of his early adulthood, Foreman had blossomed into a profoundly spiritual mature adult. After a loss in 1977 to Pedro Agosto in Puerto Rico, Foreman went back to his dressing room and nearly died from exhaustion and heatstroke. As he teetered on the edge of death, Big George begged God to save him, and when his life was spared, he dedicated himself to serving God. For more than a decade, Foreman was minister of a small church in Houston.

Tenacity? The hand of God? All of these certainly played a part. But I feel that the events of that night in Las Vegas, a night when he lost what many considered to be his only chance at regaining a title, set the tone for a man who could not help but triumph. Foreman's unwillingness to shift responsibility for his performance onto someone else, however justified, spoke to his soul and shouted to the world that George Foreman was not a victim. Regardless of what transpired, he was master of his fate and he was not going to point the finger of blame at anyone.

George Foreman did not excuse his poor performance.

When you are faced with a person complaining to excuse his or her poor performance, know that attempting to point out that person's culpability in what transpired is futile. So too is trying to point out any advantages the person had and/or missed. What has happened has already happened and cannot be changed. The best thing you can do to help the person shift focus and stop complaining is to ask what he or she plans to do the next time.

When someone complains to Excuse poor performance, ask what he or she plans to do differently next time.

"The sun was in my eyes."

"What can you do next time to be prepared in case the sun is in your eyes again?"

"The air was dry, my throat was sore, and so I couldn't sing as well as I would have liked."

"Sometimes you'll be singing where the air is dry. What can you do to be ready?"

"You didn't wake me up."

"Sometimes I might forget. What can you do to make sure you get out of bed on your own if I don't remember?"

"He didn't have the part ready, so I couldn't get my work done."

"If that happens again, what can you do to make sure the task gets completed anyway or, at least, make certain that those who need to know will be informed ahead of time?"

People complain to **G**et attention, **R**emove responsibility from themselves, **I**nspire envy, have **P**ower over others, and **E**xcuse poor performance. As you hear people complain, you will notice that sometimes the same complaint is uttered for multiple reasons. A person may complain to get attention as well as to brag. Or a person may complain to gain power and, simultaneously, to excuse poor performance. By familiarizing yourself with the strategies presented in this chapter, you'll prepare yourself to combine your responses as needed for optimal effect. The proper combination of these approaches will assure that the person ceases to bring his or her gripes to you.

One final suggestion on getting others to stop complaining that has been used with great success by many people is to create a Complaint Free Zone.

The idea is simple. In the back of our free Complaint Free Kids curriculum and our Complaint Free Organizations program, both of which are available free from our website, www.AComplaintFreeWorld.org, there is a sign you can post that looks like this:

COMPLAINING

**THIS AREA IS HEREBY DESIGNATED
AN OFFICIAL COMPLAINT FREE ZONE.**

IF YOU WISH TO:

- COMPLAIN
- CRITICIZE
- GOSSIP

PLEASE STEP AWAY TO SOMEWHERE ELSE.

Download our sign or create your own. Post the sign where people tend to congregate: the break room at work, the kitchen in your home, the car, your living room, a meeting room, your cubicle—anywhere that people come together and you've noticed a tendency toward griping. You don't need to make a formal announcement about this, and you don't need others' permission to establish a Complaint Free Zone (chances are, you won't get it). Simply do it.

Then, when someone begins to complain, take that person

gently by the arm and lead him or her out of the Complaint Free Zone.

"Hey, what's going on?" the person will ask.

You respond, "We were in a Complaint Free zone. It sounded to me like you were complaining, so I thought I'd guide you out of the zone so you can say what you wanted to say."

This is a fun, subtle, and yet powerful way to delicately point out the other person's negativity, and in most cases, raising that person's awareness is enough to get him or her to complain less overall. Remember that just as you have found it unnerving to realize how often you complain, others will probably have the same reaction to their own complaining.

> The best way to get others to stop complaining is through redirection rather than confrontation.

The best way to get others to stop complaining is through redirection rather than confrontation. When you train yourself through persistent practice to use these techniques, you will find that you are able to retrain others who complain to you. Before we leave the topic of getting others to stop complaining, consider helping your entire town or city to become Complaint Free. This is much easier than you might think. Get your city council or mayor's office to declare the day before Thanksgiving Complaint Free Wednesday. Appendix A of this book tells you how, and Appendix B includes a sample resolution and suggested press release.

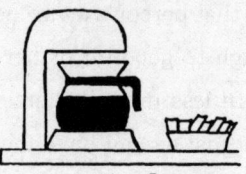

No complaining!
$100 fine for each violation.

Browman

Deprived of her favorite means of expression, Kathy was speechless--much to the relief of her coworkers.

CHAPTER 5

WAKING UP

The Indian knew how to live without wants,
to suffer without complaint, and to die singing.

—ALEXIS DE TOCQUEVILLE

A young monk entered an order that mandated total silence. At his discretion, the abbot could allow any monk to speak. It was nearly five years before the abbot approached the novice and said, "You may now speak two words."

Choosing his words carefully, the monk said, "Hard bed." With genuine concern the abbot said, "I'm sorry your bed isn't comfortable. We'll see if we can get you another one."

Another half decade passed before the abbot came to the young monk and said, "You may say two more words."

After a few moments' deliberation, the monk said softly, "Cold food."

"We'll see what we can do," replied the abbot.

On the monk's fifteenth anniversary, the abbot allowed the monk to speak two words as before.

VOICES

I was recently traveling and bad weather had surrounded some of the destination airports, causing many flights to get canceled or delayed. I was sitting by the gate, having changed my flight to another one already, and was watching the unfortunate airline rep at the gate counter. She was being bombarded by a number of people who seemed to assume that the poor weather, flight cancellations, and everything else causing them grief was her fault, and each one in turn laid all of their grief on her and I could see she was being pushed to the brink.

A little aha lightbulb flashed in my mind, and since I am apt to follow my instinct, I stood up and took my place in the line of people intent on sharing their bad day with her. I patiently waited my turn, and when I was finally standing in front of her, her weary eyes looked up to me, her forehead creased with stress, and she asked, "May I help you, sir?"

I said "Yes you can." I then asked her to act busy while I spoke to her. I told her I stood in line to give her a five-minute break. While she typed (I have no idea what she typed), I explained to her that while all of these people were intent on ruining her day, she had other people in her life who really cared about her and passions in her life that gave her life meaning, and this was far more important than what was

happening here today. Given all of that, the stuff hap-
pening here wasn't important and shouldn't stress her
out. We chatted back and forth for a few minutes as she
continued to look busy.

After seeing her regain her composure, I knew she
had to get back to her work and I wished her a great
day, telling her it was time for the next customer. She
looked up at me and I could see that her eyes were
slightly welling up. "Thank you so much," she said. "I
don't know how to thank you for this."

I smiled and told her the best way to thank me was
to pass on the kindness to someone else when she had
the opportunity.

—HARRY TUCKER,

NEW YORK, NEW YORK

"I quit," said the monk.

"It's probably for the best," replied the abbot with a shrug.
"You've done nothing but gripe since you got here."

Like the young monk, you probably had not realized how
often you complain, but by now you are awakening to the
truth about yourself.

We've all experienced sitting, leaning, or lying on an arm
or leg for a period of time and having it "fall asleep." When we

shift our weight and the blood rushes back into the limb, it tingles. Sometimes the tingle is uncomfortable, even painful. The same is true when you begin to wake up to your complaining nature. If you're like most people, realizing how often you complain can be shocking. That's okay. Just keep moving that bracelet and stay with it. Don't give up.

In Chapter 2, I mentioned that I was very overweight as a child. In my senior year of high school, I lost in excess of one hundred pounds. When friends asked what diet had achieved such great results for me, I answered honestly, "The one I stuck with." I had been on dozens of diets but finally stayed with one and trimmed down.

> "Success is going from failure to failure without losing enthusiasm."
>
> —WINSTON CHURCHILL

So stick with your commitment to become Complaint Free even when you're shocked and embarrassed at how often you complain. Stick with it when you feel justified in complaining. Stick with it when you crave the opportunity to paint yourself as a victim and gain sympathy from others. Most important, stick with it even when you accumulate several Complaint Free days, stumble, and complain. Even if you're on Day 20, switch your bracelet and start anew. That's all it takes, starting over again and again— moving that bracelet. In the words of Winston Churchill, "Success is going from failure to failure without losing enthusiasm."

One of my hobbies is juggling. I learned to juggle from a book that came with three square-shaped bags filled with crushed pecan shells. The bag's shape and contents were designed to keep the bags from rolling away when they were dropped. The implicit message behind the design was: We are *going* to be dropped.

For years I juggled at my daughter's school functions and other events, but I always decline invitations to juggle at talent shows. Juggling is not a talent; it's a skill. A talent can be cultivated and nurtured to full expression. A skill is something most people can learn if they are willing to invest enough time.

When I juggle, people will often say, "I wish I could do that."

"You can," I respond. "Just put in the time."

"No," they often say, "I'm not coordinated enough." This comment removes them from the responsibility of trying and putting forth the effort to become proficient at a skill I'm convinced nearly anyone can master.

When they hear about the Complaint Free Challenge, many people say the same thing: "I wish I could do that, but I can't."

Nonsense. Becoming Complaint Free is a skill like learning to juggle. A person must simply put forth the effort a little at a time, and just like Mike Carmichael's ball of paint, soon they will have something amazing.

I've taught several people to juggle, and I always begin by handing them one of the non-rolling bags with an instruction to drop the bag on the floor.

"Now pick it up," I say. My students do.

"Now drop it again." Again, they comply.

"Good! Now pick it up."

"Drop it."

"Pick it up."

"Drop it."

"Pick it up."

We'll go through this many times until the person begins to tire of the whole exercise and asks, "What does this have to do with learning to juggle?"

"Everything," I say. "If you want to learn to juggle, you have to be prepared to drop the balls and pick them up thousands of times. But if you stay with it," I assure the student, "you *can* juggle."

Just keep picking up the balls. Pick them up and start over even when you're tired and frustrated. Pick them up when people laugh at you. Pick them up when it seems like you juggled for a shorter time than the last time you dropped them. Just keep picking them up.

Every time I've mastered a new juggling maneuver, it's been back to dropping and picking up again. The first time I tried to juggle clubs, I spun one club in the air, and its wooden handle smashed hard into my collarbone, raising a painful welt. I threw the clubs in a closet, deciding I could never learn to juggle them.

A person who puts his or her purple bracelet in a drawer is making certain that he or she will not become Complaint Free. With my clubs collecting dust in the closet, there was no way I'd learn to juggle them. A year later, I hauled them out and tried again.

Being careful to avoid the hard handles as they spun in my direction, I tried to keep three clubs in the air, dropping them repeatedly. However, because I stayed with it, I can now juggle not only clubs but also knives and even flaming torches.

Anyone who is willing to pick up the balls, clubs, knives, or torches over and over again can learn to juggle. Anyone willing to switch his or her bracelet and start over, and over and over, can become a Complaint Free person.

You may question whether what you say is a complaint or a statement of fact. Remember the difference between a complaint and a statement of fact is the energy you put into your comment. According to Dr. Robin Kowalski, "Whether or not the particular statement reflects a complaint . . . depends on whether the speaker is experiencing an internal dissatisfaction." The words in a complaint and a noncomplaint can be identical; what distinguishes the two is your meaning, your energy behind them. The Conscious Incompetent stage is all about becoming aware of what you say and, more important, the energy behind what you're saying.

Remember, there is no prize for being the fastest person to complete the twenty-one-day challenge. In fact, I tend to be skeptical of people who say they have been at it for a week and are already on Day 7. In my experience, these are people who are not aware when they complain. They may have donned the bracelet, but they are still lingering in the Unconscious Incompetent stage.

In my experience, those who are really making progress are like the woman who posted today on our Facebook page (www.facebook.com/AComplaintFreeWorld): "Got my bracelets 10 minutes ago . . . already had to change it around 5 times." An hour later she posted, "I'm up to 10 times!"

> "Habit is habit, and not to be flung out of the window by any man, but coaxed downstairs a step at a time."
>
> —MARK TWAIN

I commented simply, "Hang in there, you're on the right track."

Becoming Complaint Free is not a race. It's not a magic pill. It's a process of transformation. It's unlearning and adopting a whole new way of being. It's leaving behind a deeply ingrained habit. And this takes time.

Becoming a Complaint Free person is ceasing to rail against that which cannot be changed. As I write this, I'm sitting in the train station in San Jose, California. My train was scheduled to leave at 9 A.M. but has not shown up to the depot. The time is now 10:30, and I've just been informed that the new departure time is 12 P.M.—three hours late. Depending on how you read what I've just written, you might think I'm complaining.

For myself, I know my energy about the situation. I am sitting on the train platform, enjoying the spring morning and a cup of cinnamon spice tea while typing on my laptop, sharing something about which I am passionate. I am happy. I am grateful for the morning. The train leaving late is a wonderful gift because it has given me more time to write. I get to do what I love in a beautiful environment.

Hmm, but what if I don't want to wait. Perhaps if I complain loudly and angrily to the ticket agent or if I complain to everyone seated around me, maybe I could get the train to leave sooner. That would work, right?

Of course not.

And yet we see people do this all the time. The train will get here when it's supposed to and it will be the perfect time.

I was recently interviewed by a radio morning show. One of the announcers said, "But I complain for a living—and I get paid very well for complaining."

"Okay," I said, "and on a scale of one to ten, how happy are you?"

After a beat he said, "Is there a negative number?"

Complaining may benefit us in many ways, such as gaining sympathy and attention—it may even gain us a radio audience—but being happy is not a benefit derived from complaining.

And you deserve to be happy, to have the material possessions you want, to have friendships and relationships that fill your heart and satisfy your desires. You deserve to be healthy and to have a career you enjoy.

Take this in: Anything you desire, you deserve.

Stop making excuses and begin to move toward your dreams. If you are saying things like "Men are commitment-phobic," "Everyone in my family is fat," "I'm not coordinated," or "My high school guidance counselor told me I'd never amount to anything," you are making yourself a victim. Victims don't become victors. And you get to choose which you will be.

Complaining is like a note from Epstein's mother. Remember the show *Welcome Back, Kotter*? Juan Epstein, one of the students in this 1970s classroom comedy, would often bring notes to school to get out of doing things he didn't want to do. A note might read, "Epstein can't take the test today because he was up all night discovering a cure for cancer. Signed, Epstein's Mother." Of course Epstein wrote the notes himself to avoid doing schoolwork. We complain to get ourselves out of taking risks and doing things we don't want to do. The complaints seem legitimate, but they're thin excuses, and like the notes on the show, they're actually written by the character presenting them: us.

Please know that I understand you may have had some unfortunate and painful things happen to you. Many of us have. You can tell the story about these events forever, be "right" about what happened, and let this be an excuse that limits you your entire life. Or you can remember the slingshot.

What determines how far a stone will fly from a slingshot? The answer is: how far back you've pulled the band. If you study the lives of successful people, you will find that their success occurred not in spite of their life challenges but often *because* of them. They stopped telling everyone how much they were wronged and began to seek ways of turning the manure of their lives into fertilizer for their growth and success. Their slingshot was pulled back far, but as a result, they soared even farther.

Freida Nicholson Woodroof was born at home in a little farmhouse in Sedgwick County, Kansas, in 1928.

Although Freida grew to be a slight woman barely five feet tall, she was exquisitely proportioned and strikingly beautiful. From an early age, she received constant attention from men of all ages. "The fellows just wouldn't leave me alone," she says today with a playful smile. "But you know, I really liked the attention."

On August 27, 1966, Freida was driving her '63 Chevy down a county highway. An unseasonably cool front had chilled the typically sweltering midwestern summer down to a pleasant seventy-two degrees. Freida had spent the morning helping paint a day-care center, and the wind blowing through the open car window dried the drops of paint on her hands. Freida felt fulfilled, giddy, as high and free as the feathery clouds that meandered above her through the vast Missouri sky.

The afternoon was hers, and Freida debated whether or not to return home to await a call from her daughter, who had earlier that day married a soldier from Camp Lejeune, North Carolina. Or, perhaps, she might swing by her friend Ada's home to have a cup of coffee and share her joy over her daughter's marriage. In the end, Freida decided to go home and wait for the call from her daughter. She reasoned that she could go to Ada's house after talking to her daughter and would have that much more to share in their conversation.

As Freida approached the Arley Methodist Church, she saw something that took a moment to comprehend. Rounding the curve ahead and barreling down on her was a young man in a large red car. In a tenth of a second her mind vaulted from "What's happening?" to "He'll see he's in the wrong lane and pull back" to "Oh no, this is it!"

Freida jerked the steering wheel violently to the right, forcing her car into a narrow, deep ditch just as the red car and its oblivious driver passed. Pressing the brakes with all her might, she simultaneously twisted the wheel sharply to the left in an attempt to maneuver her car back onto the road. The sudden deceleration, combined with the sharp turn of the wheel and multiplied by her forward momentum, caused the car to flip repeatedly.

Few 1963 vehicles had seat belts. Even fewer drivers used them. Time became a glacier. Freida slid quickly to the passenger side of the bench seat to avoid being impaled by the steering wheel. The one-and-a-quarter-ton Chevrolet bounced and somersaulted like an angry, wounded beast.

The steering wheel Freida had so nimbly avoided viciously tore all the way through the driver's seat she had occupied less than a second before.

Freida's face slammed once, twice, three times into the windshield, knocking her senseless but not unconscious.

After seconds that seemed like hours the glacier of time began to melt and the car began to settle. Freida's small, delicate body, now jostled and broken, slipped through the hole where the passenger window had been. Her torso was free, but her hips and legs remained trapped within in the confines of the wreckage. Freida's face hit the glass-strewn ground with a sickening thud.

"I'm not dead," she thought through the backdoor haze of her scrambled mind. "If I'm not dead, I'll be all right."

But there was one last bit of energy yet to be expelled in the crash. Groaning like a monstrous dying bull the mangled Chevrolet shuddered, creaked, and slowly rolled over one final time, coming to rest on Freida's small head.

Still, she remained conscious.

The weight of the car crushed Freida's once beautiful face into the dirt. She was awake and badly injured, but her thoughts were not on her injuries. They were consumed with forcing her body to draw in enough breath to remain alive.

What was left of her nose was smashed and unusable and her mouth was pinched nearly closed, but Freida forced her lungs to suck hard to pull air through a space no larger than a pencil lead. Each inhalation and each exhalation took nearly a full minute. Her mind was wild with panic.

"We've got to get her out of there!" a man's voice said from what seemed a thousand miles away.

"Run borrow the Rachle brothers' tractor!" another screamed.

Freida gave no thought to her rescue. She was consumed with trying to breathe.

It seemed an eternity before Freida felt more than heard the throb of the diesel engine of the approaching tractor. As the tractor's hydraulic lift hefted the car back onto its wheels, Freida's limp body tumbled to the ground. She was consumed not with pain but with the ecstasy of drawing a full breath for the first time since the accident.

Her face crushed, her beautiful blue left eye now dangling from its socket, the once fair Freida looked frightful. Fully in shock but still fully awake, she heard from the edges of consciousness commentary from the bevy of onlookers who had gathered.

"Oh my God!" said one.

"She used to be so pretty!" said another.

"It's a good thing she got married and had children when she was young!" interjected a third.

The ambulance had to travel nearly forty miles to come for Freida. Unable to speak, her skull and face crushed, she lay in the ditch wondering when she would lose consciousness.

She never did.

Hours later she arrived at the hospital. Because she had sustained a head injury, the doctors refused Freida pain medication for an excruciating twenty-four hours. A compassionate nurse named, ironically, Mrs. Love sat with Freida around the clock and held her hand. The pain was a scorching wildfire burning though Freida's body. She would have screamed had she the facial structure to scream with. She clutched Mrs. Love's hand, and the nurse spoke softly and gently, encouraging Freida to just hold on.

When the initial twenty-four hours was over and she could at last have pain medicine, Freida slept a very long time. She awakened to the sensation of her children's tears gently falling on her hand.

When at last her mangled face had been wired somewhat back together, Freida croaked out her first words since the accident. "I forgive him," she said, and she slipped back into unconsciousness.

In total, twenty-two reconstructive surgeries contributed to rebuilding Freida's face. She now has a crooked little Mona Lisa smile that seems more sly and mirthful than the result of a horrendous car accident. Her prosthetic eye is a perfect match for the remaining one, and both twinkle with equal brilliance.

Freida observed her eighty-third birthday last week, and it was my pleasure to take her to lunch to celebrate. You would never guess her to be an octogenarian by the way she bounds with contagious energy when she walks and lights up any room she enters.

What would have forever ruined the life of most people was just a speed bump to Freida.

"I know you forgave the driver of the red car," I said, "but don't you hold some resentment for how the accident changed you?"

Freida's perpetual smile widened, "Changed me?" she said. "It didn't change me. I'm still the same person. I've always felt beautiful inside."

Freida continues to have a full life nearly five decades after the accident. She built a successful small business, raised her children, and enjoys life to the fullest. She will tell you that, if anything, the accident helped her understand the truth of who she is, which is far more than just another pretty face.

"I've got at least twenty-two good years left in me," she told me, "and I plan to enjoy them to the fullest."

When something traumatic happens in our lives, we have a choice to let it defeat us or to let it complete us.

> "The measure of mental health is the disposition to find good everywhere."
>
> —RALPH WALDO EMERSON

It can be a fire that consumes us or a fire that refines us.

It can be a tragic last act or a joyous new beginning.

PART 3

CONSCIOUS COMPETENCE

CHAPTER 6

SILENCE AND THE LANGUAGE OF COMPLAINING

We are what we repeatedly do.
Excellence, then, is not an act but a habit.

—ARISTOTLE

The Conscious Competence stage is one of hypersensitivity. In it, you begin to be aware of everything you say. You are moving your bracelet far less frequently because you are very careful when you speak. You are now talking in more positive terms because you are beginning to catch your words before they come out of your mouth. Your

"Before speaking, consider whether it is an improvement upon silence."

—SWAMI KRIPALVANANDJI

purple bracelet has gone from being a tool for recognizing when you complain to being a filter through which your words pass before you speak them.

VOICES

I got my purple bracelet and was determined to not complain, criticize or gossip.

I went out to lunch with a friend of mine. When she started talking about things that were "wrong" and wanted me to agree with her, I pulled up my sleeve and showed her my purple bracelet and told her what I was attempting to do.

She said, "Well then, what are we going to talk about?"

That was a very awkward moment. I said, "I don't know." Then I started saying how good the food was that we were eating, and how beautiful the flowers were across the street.

I think I would have been a little put off too, if someone said that to me in the middle of a conversation. But it's getting easier for me, whether I tell my friends/relatives or not. I just change the subject or try to lighten up the conversation. (Or say "Excuse me, I have to go to the bathroom.")

—JOAN MCCLURE,

FORT BRAGG, CALIFORNIA

One family who took the Complaint Free challenge e-mailed that everyone in the family seemed to hit the Conscious Competent stage at the same time. "For about a week we just sat at the dinner table and stared at each other, afraid to speak," the father told me.

Prolonged periods of silence are typical for a person in the Conscious Competent stage. You learn the simple profundity of a mother's perennial advice: "If you can't say anything nice, don't say anything at all."

Before our bracelets were custom-made bearing our logo, we purchased them from a novelty company that sold them as "Spirit" bracelets. If your school color was green, you would order green school spirit bracelets; red spirit bracelets for schools with red as their color.

Once we began to have our bracelets custom-made, we kept the word SPIRIT for a while embossed on the side opposite our logo. We did this because we discovered that the word "spirit" comes from the Latin *spiritus* and means "breath." In the Conscious Competent stage, one of the best things you can do is to draw a deep breath rather than speaking out of hand. Complaining is a habit, and taking a moment just to breathe gives you a chance to select your words more carefully. As a reminder to take a breath rather than complain, for a time we kept the word "spirit."

> "Smile, breathe, and go slowly."
>
> —THICH NHAT HANH

We finally dropped SPIRIT from the bracelets because many people saw the word "spirit" and made the understandable assumption that we were somehow instructing people to be more spiritual or religious. A Complaint Free World is a nonreligious human transformation movement.

Spiritus—to breathe. When you find yourself around other people who are complaining and you catch yourself feeling compelled to chime in, breathe. When something frustrating happens and you have the chance to unload your frustrations on someone else, breathe.

Breathe. Breathe and be silent.

Silence affords the opportunity to choose to speak from your higher self rather than your human self. Silence is a bridge to the Infinite, and yet it is something with which many are uncomfortable. I can remember being at our lake house when I was a teenager and canoeing over to a small island about a mile from our home to camp alone. The silence gave me a chance to reconnect with myself.

"Do everything without complaining."

—PHILIPPIANS 2:14

One afternoon, as I was paddling out toward the island, I heard my father calling to me from the bank of the lake.

"Will!"

"Yes, sir."

"Where are you going?"

"Camping over at Counts Island."

"By yourself?"

"Yes, sir."

(After a moment's pause.) "Do you want a battery-powered TV to take with you?"

"No, sir . . . thank you."

(Another pause; longer this time) "A radio?!"

"No, thanks."

My dad stood for moment, then shrugged his shoulders, turned, and walked back to the house. I love my dad, but he's not much for silence. He sleeps with a big-screen TV blaring from the foot of his bed.

If you are a person who likes to pray, the Conscious Competent stage is a good time to deepen your prayer life. You've reached a point where you really don't want to move your bracelet, so take a breath, and in that moment of silence say a little prayer before speaking. Ask for guidance that your words will be constructive rather than destructive. And, if no words come at all, remain silent. It's better to remain silent than to have to start the twenty-one-day challenge over at Day 1.

> "Even a fool, when he holdeth his peace, is counted wise: and he that shutteth his lips is esteemed a man of understanding."
>
> —PROVERBS 17:28

Back when I was a young man selling radio advertising, I worked with a man who talked infrequently, if at all. After getting to know him, I asked why he sat without talking in meetings while others droned on incessantly. He said, "If I'm quiet, people assume that I'm smarter than I am." If you simply say nothing, people may at least give you credit for being smart. When we run off at the mouth, we don't make ourselves sound intelligent, we simply say that we're not comfortable enough with ourselves to let quiet reign, if even for a moment.

One of the ways we know we've met a person who is special to us is the amount of time we can be with that person with no words being spoken. We're simply comfortable in their presence and enjoy their company, and a lot of mindless jabbering doesn't improve our time with them, it makes it less precious.

Silence allows you to reflect and to carefully select your words, to speak of things you wish to put your creative energy toward rather than allowing your discomfort to cause you to spout off a laundry list of grievances.

This stage of becoming Complaint Free was described in an e-mail we received from a lieutenant colonel at the Pentagon:

> *A quick update on how we're doing. All twelve bracelets are distributed among my coworkers, and so far there is one gal (who has always been quiet and low key) who is having some great success. I think she actually got into double digits!*
>
> *The rest of us, however, are finding it more difficult than we even imagined. It HAS done something very important for us, though . . .*

*when we are complaining, we know about it, we pause, we move
our bracelets, and we restate what we were saying more positively.
I haven't even gone an entire day yet, but I can see what a powerful
communication tool it is for the synergy of an office. We are able
to laugh at ourselves when we're complaining and challenge each
other to find a better way. I'll send another update when someone
reaches their goal. (Everyone is excited about expanding the challenge to more folks here in the Pentagon, so we're moving forward.)
Have a Great Air Force Day!*

—CATHY HAVERSTOCK

I mentioned before that the words you use when complaining often will be the same as the words you use when you are
not. It is your intention and your energy behind what you say
that determine whether or not you are complaining. Begin to
notice how often and in what context you say the following:

- "Of course!"
- "Wouldn't you know it?"
- "Just my luck!"
- "This always happens to me!"

When something goes wrong and you say "Of course!" or
"Wouldn't you know it?" you are sending out a message that
bad things are expected for you. The Universe responds to
your statements by sending you more problems and chal-

lenges. The best barometer of whether or not you are a positive person is how you use the words "of course."

I can remember the first time I decided to watch what I said very carefully, knowing that it was a reflection of my thoughts and that my thoughts create my reality. I borrowed a twenty-year-old pickup truck to retrieve some things I had in storage. This old F-150 had several hundred thousand miles on its original engine and got about twenty miles to the gallon— of oil! I had to stop repeatedly to add oil and carried a case of thirty-weight in the truck bed.

> The best barometer of whether or not you are a positive person is how you use the words "of course."

As I left to retrieve my belongings, a trip of a hundred-plus miles, I made sure the oil reservoir was filled and invited my dog Gibson to ride in the cab to keep me company.

It took several hours to drive from my home in Aynor, South Carolina, to the storage unit in Manning, South Carolina, and load up my belongings. As Gibson and I drove back, I decided to take a shortcut and headed down some two-lane country roads toward Greeleyville, South Carolina. I used to live in Manning and knew the route to Greeleyville well. In fact, I used to ride my bike to Greeleyville and back on weekends for exercise because it was a stretch of about thirteen miles one-way with little traffic.

I had been meticulously checking and adding oil to the old truck, but as the sun began to set, the CHECK ENGINE light came on. As was my habit, my mind went to "Oh, no! I'm in trouble," but I caught myself. I remembered my commitment to monitor and control my thoughts.

I turned to Gibson, who lay dozing on the seat next to me, and said, "This is going to work out perfectly." Inside, I thought I was a little crazy. Not for talking to a dog, but for thinking that I would somehow make it home in this dilapidated old truck driving down deserted country roads. As I said, I knew this stretch of road well. In the thirteen miles there were only a dozen or so homes scattered sporadically along the road, and I was not carrying a cell phone.

The truck sputtered and spat but continued on for about a mile, until suddenly the engine died. Through gritted teeth I said, "This is going to work out fine," attempting to convince myself. The truck began to slow and finally glided to a stop directly in front of someone's home.

"Of course!" I said to myself and to Gibson, celebrating the moment and yet still amazed at how fortunate we had been. "Maybe the people who live here are at home and they'll let me use their phone." I reasoned that I could call someone to come and pick us up, and leave the truck at the side of the road until I could have it repaired.

Then I remembered the truck bed loaded with my belongings and said aloud, "No. I would rather be able to drive home tonight and not have to leave my things at the side of the road. I don't know how this is going to work out, but I'm going to believe it is. I see myself parked in my driveway tonight, in this truck with all my stuff."

Now, remember, this was not my typical way of thinking. In the past, I would have gotten out of the truck and probably done something helpful like swear or kick the tires. Instead, I closed my eyes and visualized Gibson and me pulling into the driveway. In my mental picture, it was evening—just as it was at that time—and I was in the same clothes I was currently wearing. I allowed myself to sit a moment and clearly take this image in before walking up the driveway and ringing the doorbell.

When I heard people stirring inside the house, I smiled and said again, "Of course!" giving thanks that the people in this, the only house I could see for miles, were home just at the moment the truck stopped working. A man answered, and we exchanged introductions. When I explained that my truck had broken down and asked if I might use his phone, he peered past me into the darkness and asked, "What kind of truck are you driving?"

"A Ford," I said.

He smiled. "I'm the service manager at the Ford truck dealership. Let me get my tools and take a look."

"Of course!" I said again as he went to get his tools. I was positively giddy with excitement. Not only had our truck broken down directly in front of someone's house on a desolate stretch of road, but the man who lived there was responsible for all the repairs for a hundred miles or more on trucks of the very make I was driving.

Wow!

I held a flashlight for him as the man tinkered under the hood for about fifteen min-

> "Believe as a child believes and the magic will find you."
>
> —TERESA LANGDON

utes. He finally turned and said, "The problem is that there is something wrong with your fuel system. You need a small part. Doesn't cost but a dollar or two, but I don't have one here at my house.

"What you've got," he continued, "is more of a plumbing problem than a mechanical problem."

"That's okay," I said with a shrug. "Maybe I can just use your phone, then?"

"Well," he said, "you've got a plumbing problem, and my father is visiting from Kentucky. My dad's a plumber. I'll go get him."

As the man trotted back to the house to retrieve his father, I scrubbed the fur on Gibson's neck and, smiling deliriously, said, "Of course!"

A few minutes later the man's father had diagnosed the truck's problem.

"You need a piece of tubing about three inches long and one-quarter-inch wide," he said.

"Like this one?" his son said, pulling a tube of that exact size from his own toolbox.

"That's it!" said the father. "Where did you find one?"

"I don't know where it came from," his son said. "I found it on my workbench a month or so ago and just dropped it in the toolbox in case I ever needed it."

Of course!

Five minutes later Gibson and I were back on the road. "What an experience," I said to Gibson, who was now excitedly poking his head out of the passenger's window.

It *had* worked out. We were on our way. I would be pulling into the driveway that very night with my belongings.

But at that precise moment the OIL light lit up the dash. We had sat for so long in front of the man's home that the oil had drained from the truck, and it was dangerously low. Before leaving the warehouse facility, I had poured the last quart I had into the oil reserve.

Seeing no homes ahead, I began to get concerned, but then stopped myself, saying loudly, "It worked once, it can work again!" As I drove, I again called forth the image of us pulling safely into our driveway that very night.

Turning the corner into Greeleyville, I pulled into what was then the only gas station in town. The owner was locking the door for the night.

"Can I help you?" he asked.

"I need oil," I said.

Switching the station lights back on, he said, "Get what you need." As I walked toward the shelf that held the quarts of oil, I shoved my hands into my pants pockets and pulled out all the money I was carrying. At the rate the truck was dropping oil, I knew I might need about four quarts just to make it home. Quickly counting my money, I realized that I had only $4.56 with me. I grabbed two quarts, which was all I could afford, and laid them on the counter.

"Did you see the other brand?" the owner asked.

"No," I said.

He began walking toward the shelves, and I followed.

"There!" he said. "It's a good brand, better I think than the one you picked out, but I'm not going to carry it anymore, so we just put it on sale today—half price." Happy to the point of elation but not wanting to seem mentally unbalanced, I swept four quarts of the oil up into my arms and walked briskly to the counter. At 11:17 that very night, Gibson and I pulled safely into our driveway.

How did that happen? What celestial maneuverings took place? What realignment of possibilities and probabilities transpired to facilitate this miracle? And how in the world did it work?

The answer to this question is "WHO CARES?" It happened, and it happens time and again when we have the courage to believe. The future is not set, and to complain about present circumstances serves only to carry undesirable conditions forward.

One of the questions I'm often asked is "But don't you need to complain to get what you want?" You can get what you desire best by expressing what you want rather than complaining about how things are.

"He does not believe who does not live according to his belief."

—THOMAS FULLER

A while back, my cell phone rang and the caller ID read "Unknown Caller." I was busy, so I didn't answer. The caller didn't leave a message. An hour later I received a call from the same number, identified again on my screen as "Unknown Caller," which I also ignored. Soon I received another call, and then another, and later another. Before the day was out, "Unknown Caller" was ringing my phone approximately once each hour. I never answered these calls and the caller never left a message.

Later that evening, feeling frustrated by the incessant calls, I answered "Unknown Caller's" call and heard a recorded message from my cell phone company: "This is an important message for Mary Johnson [not her real name]. . . . If you are Mary, press one. If you are not this person, press three."

Happy to now know what all the calls were about, and in

an effort to stop them from continuing, I pressed three on my telephone keypad.

And yet the calls continued. Fifteen minutes later I answered to hear the same recorded message. As before, I pressed three to inform the phone company that I was *not* Mary Johnson and hoping they would catch their error and stop the calls.

The calls didn't stop. Every time I answered, I got the same friendly computerized message. I pressed three each time, but the calls continued.

People make mistakes. I know I do. And companies are just large groups of people doing the best they can. So, after several days of these hourly calls, I dialed the cell phone company, explained the situation, and the customer service representative assured me that the calls would stop.

The calls continued.

Prior to my making the twenty-one consecutive days Complaint Free, I probably would have called the company again, asked for a supervisor, and ripped into that poor soul. Further, I would have told everyone I came in contact with what a terrible injustice this was and how I had been greatly inconvenienced.

Instead, I called again and spoke to a customer service representative. "I know mistakes happen, and I know this isn't your fault," I said. "I'm committed to not getting these calls from your company anymore and want to work with you until we find the reason and fix it together." Within ten minutes, she found the issue (they had input my number in their database as this woman's) and the calls ceased.

I was able to get the result I wanted without having to raise my blood pressure or get angry. I also did not involve my friends, coworkers, and family in this issue by griping to them about it. Instead, I went to someone who could help me, explained what I wanted, and held that intention until it was realized.

The shortest path to get what you desire is not to talk about or focus on the problem. Focus *beyond* the problem. Talk only about what you desire, and only to someone who can provide the solution. You will shorten the wait time for what you seek, and be happier in the process.

"But every great thing in our country began with people complaining. . . . Think about Thomas Jefferson and Martin Luther King!" an e-mail I received stated.

I realized that in one respect I agreed with the woman who sent this e-mail. The first step toward progress is dissatisfaction. But if we stay in dissatisfaction, we never move forward to brighter vistas. And those who complain as a matter of course chart their destination to be the same unhappy port from which they sailed. Our focus must be on what we want to occur rather than on what we don't want to happen. Complaining focuses our intention on what we don't want to occur.

Jefferson and King both pointed out our nation's dissatisfaction with prevailing conditions, but they did not leave it there. They painted a picture of what could be. Their dissatisfaction drove them to envision the predominant challenges fully resolved, and their passion for these visions inspired others to follow. Their relentless focus on a bright future raced the collective heartbeat of the nation. They lived the words of another great American, Robert Kennedy: "There are those that look at things the way they are, and ask why? I dream of things that never were, and ask why not?"

> "There are those that look at things the way they are, and ask why? I dream of things that never were, and ask why not?"
>
> —ROBERT KENNEDY

Complainers ask, "Why?"

Complaint Free people ask, "Why not?"

On August 28, 1963, more than two hundred thousand Americans marched on Washington demanding equal rights. At this historic event, Reverend Dr. Martin Luther King, Jr., stood on the steps of the Lincoln Memorial, his words casting a spell over the assembled mass. King identified the problem. He said, "America has given the Negro people a bad check, a check which has come back marked 'insufficient funds.'" But he did not leave his audience drowning in words of dissatisfaction. Rather, he inspired them to hope with a vision of a world yet to come.

King declared, "I have a dream!" And he then delivered what the website American Rhetoric and many others have named "the greatest speech of the twentieth century." King constructed in the minds of his listeners a world without racism. He said that he had "been to the mountaintop," and his words carried us there with him. Dr. King focused beyond the problem at hand to the resolution sought.

In the Declaration of Independence, Thomas Jefferson clearly stated the challenges the colonies were having under the governance of the British Empire. However, this document was just not a litany of gripes. Had it been, it probably would not have fired the imagination of the world and unified the colonies.

The first paragraph of the U.S. Declaration of Independence reads:

When in the Course of human events it becomes necessary for one people to dissolve the political bands which have connected them with another and to assume among the powers of the earth, the separate and equal station to which the Laws of Nature and of Nature's God entitle them . . .

For a moment, imagine you are a citizen of one of the thirteen colonies and you read those words, "the separate and *equal* station to which the Laws of Nature and of Nature's God entitle them." At the time Jefferson wrote this, England was the world's greatest superpower, and Jefferson stated without hyperbole that this fledgling and diverse band of colonies were "equal" to this political and military behemoth.

Consider the collective gasp this inspired among the colonists, followed by the resulting swell of pride and optimism. How could they ever aspire to such a lofty ideal as to be equal to England? Because "the Laws of Nature and of Nature's God entitle[d] them."

This was not complaining, this was a compelling vision for a bright future. This was focusing beyond the problems at hand to a resolution sought.

I hold a dream for such visionaries today. For most of my life I can remember hearing news of "peace talks" focused on the Middle East. As I've listened to what is discussed at these "peace talks," it appears they are more "war talks" or "if you'll stop doing this then we'll stop doing that" talks. Many U.S. presidents have brought together the leaders of the Middle East in an attempt to entice them to reconcile their differences. But the focus of

> "You cannot simultaneously prevent and prepare for war."
>
> —ALBERT EINSTEIN

these talks is on "differences," and so the progress has been and continues to be minimal at best.

What if at these peace talks the leaders of various countries got together to talk about what it will be like when peace exists between them? What if they came together to build a collective dream of peaceful cohabitation and a mutual understanding?

When these true "peace talks" occur, the rules would be simple. Rather than talking about what is going on in the present or what has happened in the past, the focus will remain exclusively on what it will be like when there is no more acrimony between these countries. The participants might ask, "What will peace between our countries look, feel, sound, and smell like? What will it be like when war and disagreement between us are such a distant memory that we would have to consult history books to know about them, because such a time is lost to us?"

The focus of the talks would be on the desired outcome—peace. That's it. At these talks one word would not be uttered: "how." The question of "How will we get there?" should be agreed upon as off limits at the outset. As soon as the two parties would attempt to divine the path to their harmonious existence, questions of geographical boundaries, remunerations, disarmament, cultural and theological differences, and opposing perspectives of all types could bring their focus back to current disagreements.

As you move through this Conscious Competent phase of your transformation, it's fine to use terms such as "Of course!" "Wouldn't you know it?" "Just my luck!" and "This always happens to me!" but only when something you perceive as good happens.

Say these phrases exclusively as exclamations of thanksgiving when things go well for you, and you will soon find more things occurring to celebrate.

I have a friend in Seattle who believes he is the luckiest guy in the world. He has a beautiful wife and family, a successful and growing business; he was a multimillionaire by age thirty and enjoys excellent health. Based on his life, you might agree that, indeed, he is lucky, but this conclusion misses the point. He has and enjoys a good life because he *believes* that he is lucky. Every morning he gets up looking for evidence that he is fortunate, and every day responds with good fortune.

> "The most important thing to remember is this: to be ready at any moment to give up what you are for what you might become."
>
> —W. E. B. DUBOIS

Now you try it. When something goes well for you, no matter how small, say "Of course!"

Our words are powerful. And when we change what we say, we begin to change our lives. About a year ago, I was driving in the passing lane on the interstate. Ahead of me was a minivan driving about ten miles *below* the speed limit. My mind began to rant, "If you're going to drive below the speed limit, stay in the right lane and let others pass!"

A few days later, I found myself in the left-hand lane behind another vehicle driving considerably below the speed limit. It was another minivan.

Over the following weeks, this situation repeated itself—slow driver + passing lane = minivan. This became a pet peeve of mine, and I talked about it to friends and family. I thought it just a clever observation that minivan drivers seemed to drive slowly in the passing lane. I noticed, however, that the more I talked about it, the more often it occurred.

Finally I began to wonder if my belief that "minivan drivers are rude and impede the flow of traffic" drew this into my experience.

There is nothing more powerful than what you believe. The dictionary defines a belief as "something one accepts to be true." A belief, therefore, is an absolute but arbitrary mental stance. Beliefs define reality, and beliefs can be changed.

> A belief is an absolute but arbitrary mental stance.

I sought a way to reframe my observations about minivans and thought of NASCAR. When there is a wreck or hazard at a NASCAR race, a pace car comes onto the track to slow all the other drivers down until it is safe to resume racing. Once the danger has passed, the pace car leaves the track.

"What if minivans are the pace cars of the interstate?" I asked myself. "Maybe they are there to slow me down so I don't get a ticket or, worse, get involved in an accident."

This seemed far-fetched. And I doubted that adopting this belief would change my experience, but even if it lowered my stress when I was slowed by a minivan, it was worth the effort.

The next time I was in the left lane behind a slow minivan, I began to give thanks for the pace cars that had arrived. "Oops, there's a pace car up ahead," I'd tell myself. "I better slow down." Soon it became habitual for me to think of minivans as pace cars, and I actually began to forget they had another description.

The interesting thing is that as I changed what I called minivans and began to appreciate these pace cars for slowing me down, I found myself stuck behind one less and less. Today, it's exceedingly rare for me to be slowed by a minivan, but when I am, I give thanks. In these cases, it doesn't change traffic, but it does change my attitude, which is where the discord resides.

By changing my mind about minivans and celebrating them as pace cars, I changed what they were for me and they became a gift rather than a challenge. If you will begin to call the people and events in your life by names that spur positive energy within you, you will find that they no longer bother you and in fact can be a real source of inspiration and growth. Change the words you use and watch your life change. For example:

INSTEAD OF	CONSIDER
Problem	Opportunity
Setback	Challenge
Enemy	Friend
Tormentor	Mentor
Pain	Discomfort
I demand	I would appreciate
I have to	I get to
Complaint	Request
Struggle	Journey
You did this	I created this

Give it a try. It may feel awkward as you begin, but watch how it changes your attitude about a person or situation. As you change, the situation will change.

> "The mind is its own place and in itself, can make a Heaven of Hell, a Hell of Heaven."
>
> —JOHN MILTON,
> *PARADISE LOST*

Remember John Milton's comment from *Paradise Lost*, "The mind is its own place and in itself, can make a Heaven of Hell, a Hell of Heaven."

When someone asks, "How are you?" I have heard people groan sarcastically, "Another day in paradise." I decided to adopt this as my own genuine answer to this question. Not as a sarcastic statement but as a sincere belief: "It's another day in paradise."

It was uncomfortable at first but has now become second nature. I've noticed that this comment makes others smile brightly, and more important, it reminds me that I have a choice in that moment to be happy or sad, to dwell in heaven or hell.

Do you know what the word "amen" means? A friend of mine said, "It's a way of closing a prayer; sort of like saying, 'Over and out, God!'"

Well, not exactly.

Amen means "and so it is." It is putting an affirmative close to what you have prayed to receive. It is a statement of faith that what you seek already is. You have released your request to the Infinite and affirm that it is so now.

Consider how powerful your words are and decide if you would say, "Amen" (and so it is) to them, intending that your words be true.

"Men cheat."
And so it is.

"Nobody likes me."
And so it is.

"That customer never buys."
And so it is.

"I'll probably die alone."
And so it is.

"I can't find a job."
And so it is.

"Life is unfair."
And so it is.

"I'll never get out of debt."
And so it is.

"I'll never find a job I love."
And so it is.

"Customer service people are rude and never really help."
And so it is.

And on and on it goes.

What you say becomes your reality. Your habitual inclination in the past may have been to say something critical, sarcastic, or negative. It takes a while to retrain yourself, and the best soil for growing the seed of a new way of speaking is silence. Take a moment to breathe and choose what you will say.

Then choose wisely.

Choose to speak what you desire rather than complaining about the way things are. And if you complain, shrug your shoulders and start again. Keep switching your bracelet with every complaint. You will succeed if you stay with it. It takes persistence to do something this important. There is an old saying: "If Columbus had turned back, no one would have blamed him. Of course, no one would have remembered him either."

> "Silence is one of the great arts of conversation."
>
> —MARCUS TULLIUS CICERO

Becoming Complaint Free is a voyage not unlike the one made by Columbus. It begins with an exciting idea of riches and great discoveries, and yet it may seem to drag on much, much too long. Don't turn back. An exciting New World awaits you.

CHAPTER 7

CRITICISM AND SARCASM

Sarcasm I now see to be, in general, the language of the devil;
for which reason I have long since as good as renounced it.

—THOMAS CARLYLE

oth criticism and sarcasm are forms of complaining.
When you engage in either, switch your bracelet.

Criticism is defined as pointing out another's faults in
a disapproving way. Therefore, "constructive criticism" is an

oxymoron. To be constructive
is to build up. To criticize is to
tear down. You are never being
constructive when you criticize someone.

"People ask for criticism,
but all they want is praise."

—W. SOMERSET MAUGHAM

No one likes to be criticized. And rather than diminishing
what we criticize, our criticism often serves to expand it.

Great leaders know that people respond much more favor-
ably to appreciation than to criticism. Appreciation inspires a

VOICES

I was doing very well with becoming Complaint Free. I had strung a series of days together and could tell it was changing my life.

My husband insisted that I stop. He said I was simply not as much fun to be around. I guess he thinks complaining is fun and I wouldn't join in with him and his griping anymore.

This makes me sad.

—NAME WITHHELD

person to excel, so as to receive more appreciation. Criticism tears people down, and people who don't feel worthwhile don't feel they can do a good job.

A vicious circle is created. A person makes a mistake and the boss criticizes. The employee feels inadequate and makes another mistake, which the boss also criticizes. This leads to more mistakes followed by criticisms followed by more mistakes.

The key is to talk not about what the person didn't do in the past, but rather about what you want the person to do in the future. Instead of "You didn't turn in your time card by 5 P.M. again! What are you, stupid?" consider "Time cards are due at 5 P.M., I'm sure you'll remember that."

Criticism is an attack. And when people are attacked, they have two options: stand and fight, or run away. They may not fight, but just because they withdraw, don't think the war is over. They will continue this or other annoying behavior as a means of counterattacking. All people seek power, and if the only way to acquire it is through passive-aggressive behavior, that's what they will do.

Attention drives behavior. As much as we'd like to feel it's the other way around, it's not true. When we criticize someone, we are inviting future demonstrations of what we are criticizing. This is true for your spouse, your children, your employees, and your friends. In George Bernard Shaw's play *Pygmalion*, Eliza Doolittle explains this phenomenon to Colonel Pickering: "You see, really and truly, apart from the things anyone can pick up (the dressing and the proper way of speaking, and so on), the difference between a lady and a flower girl is not how she behaves, but how she's treated. I shall always be a flower girl to Professor Higgins, because he always treats me as a flower girl, and always will; but I know I can be a lady to you, because you always treat me as a lady, and always will."

> "No matter the lesson, you can teach it only by instilling a sense of pride, not shame, in the pupil."
>
> —HARVEY MACKAY

We are far more powerful in the creation of our lives than we realize. Our thoughts about people determine how they will show up for us and how we will relate to them. Our words let others know our expectations of them and their behavior. If the words are critical, then the behavior will mirror the expectation represented by what we say.

We all know of parents who focus on a child's poor marks rather than celebrating the child's good grades. The child brings home a report card with four A's and a C, and the parent says, "Why did you get a C?" The focus is on the one average grade rather than on the four excellent ones.

My own daughter Lia, who had always had excellent grades, began to let her schoolwork slip at one point. When she brought home her report card, I celebrated the A's and B's and said nothing about the lower grades.

"Aren't you angry about the bad grades?" she asked.

"Why should I be angry?" I said. "They're your grades. If you're happy with them, then that's all that matters."

She wasn't happy with them, and in a very short time she brought them all up. If I had berated her for her low grades, she might have felt disempowered and angry and could have let all of her grades slip further just to show me. When I gave her the authority to decide if her grades were acceptable, she made choices that were actually beyond what I would have encouraged her to aspire to.

Leadership can be a daunting task. The use of criticism is an indication of a leader who lacks the resources to truly lead.

A leader's job is to inspire people to reach their highest

level of performance. When someone does his or her best, the organization benefits and the person experiences the satisfaction of accomplishment. The employee feels the thrill of calling forth hidden resources he or she never knew existed. People grow when they reach deep and do more, and this is exciting and stimulating for them.

A leader's job is the careful balancing of inspiration and direction.

> "The employer usually gets the employees he deserves."
>
> —J. PAUL GETTY

A while back, I was speaking at a conference, and before my speech I sat and chatted with the CEO of the sponsoring company. He had grown his business from a simple idea to a multinational, multimillion-dollar-a-year company in a just a decade. As we spoke, he told me about his company's phenomenal growth and shared what had become his greatest challenge.

"For a long time, my employees hated me," he said. "I got things done, sure, but I left people's feelings scorched by my criticisms. Our explosive growth began to plateau and then to decline."

"What did you do?" I asked.

"I had to learn to inspire people without killing their spirit," he said. "I took a trip out west just to get away, and quite by accident I learned a powerful lesson."

"What was that?" I asked.

"I took part in a cattle drive," he said. "My job was to keep the cows moving, but I found that there is a fine line between advancing the cows and scattering the herd. After pushing the cows so hard that I nearly caused a stampede, I finally asked an old-time cowboy what I was doing wrong.

"He told me that before a cow moves, it shifts its weight in the direction it plans to move. He said I should not push the cows until they moved. Just nudge them until I saw their weight shift in the direction I wanted them to go. As soon as I saw them shift their weight, I should back off."

The CEO continued, "It's a real skill to know how much pressure to apply to get the cows to shift in a certain direction and then to back off. Often I pushed too hard and a few times not hard enough; but eventually I figured it out.

"I realized that leading people is like herding cows," he said. "When I inspire them to move a certain way, and they start to move. I need to back off. What I used to do was, rather than backing off, I would feel I needed to goad them to keep going. I would explain my reasons and stress the importance of going in that direction. Even though they were going where I wanted, I pushed them out of fear they would stop. As a result, they would slow their pace and I'd criticize.

"Then they would feel disempowered and resent me," he said. "And they became less, not more, inclined to move. So now as soon as I see my people starting to go the way I want them to go, I back off."

The CEO concluded his comments with a warm smile, saying, "Now I do less than before, the company makes more money, and everyone is happier—including me."

In *Business Stripped Bare*, Sir Richard Branson writes that the key to management is to know that deep down people want to do what is best for themselves and for the organization. He writes that people are universally hard on themselves. A leader who understands this will know that even without criticism, good people will stop themselves from repeating mistakes.

For a leader in a family, civic group, church, or business, greatness lies in learning to urge people only until they show a subtle shift toward the direction you wish them to go and then to back off. This movement builds momentum and pride, which fuels more momentum. As leaders, it's not how much we do, it's how well things move forward that matters, and sometimes that is achieved by our doing less.

Sarcasm is passive-aggressive complaining.

Before you criticize people for their performance, give them a chance to correct it themselves. Chances are, they will.

Like criticism, sarcasm is also complaining. Criticism is a complaint wielded as a direct attack, whereas sarcasm is passive-aggressive complaining.

In the movie *Sling Blade*—have you figured out yet how

much I love movies? Anyway, in *Sling Blade*, country music star Dwight Yoakam plays an angry young man named Doyle. Doyle repeatedly says hurtful and even vicious things to the other characters and then waves away his cutting remarks with "Hey, I'm just kidding." The sarcastic person is a hit-and-run driver making a negative statement and then shouting over his shoulder as he speeds off, "Hey, I was just kidding!"

Sarcasm is a negative comment with a humorous escape hatch. It affords the person making the remark plausible deniability should someone call that person on it.

While working on this chapter, I posted some comments about sarcasm on Facebook. One of our Facebook fans responded, "The meaning of sarcasm is: a sharp and often satirical or ironic utterance designed to cut or give pain; a cutting, often ironic remark intended to wound. The etymology of sarcasm is even more alarming. The Latin root of sarcasm is *sarco*, which means 'tearing of the flesh.' Looking further into this, sarcasm stemmed from *sarcasmos* or *sarkazein*, which again means ripping or tearing away of the flesh. Both *sarcasmos* and *sarkazein* were forms of torture used in ancient medieval times."

As I was taking the twenty-one-day challenge, by far the hardest thing for me was to stop being sarcastic.

People ask, "What's wrong with a little sarcasm? I'm just being funny." Sarcasm is always a critical statement with a funny spin. Sarcasm is a cutting remark couched in the context of telling a joke. It's the last refuge of a person who wants to make a point but who does not want to be held responsible for any fallout that may occur as a result.

A couple of years ago, I lead a group to help build a birthing center at a hospital in Tanzania. Due to a lack of adequate medical care, some statistics cite a nearly one-in-three death rate for mothers giving birth in that poor African country.

What I found striking about the people in Africa was how friendly and happy they are. Even though many of them live in abject poverty and without proper medical care, they tend to be upbeat and cheerful.

One afternoon, our group was riding in an old tour bus to visit a museum. The side roads in Mwanza, Tanzania, are made of dirt. Large boulders, some as large as bathtubs, protrude from the ground, and drivers must weave around them. Drivers in most countries drive straight in their lanes, but drivers in Mwanza must weave sometimes all the way over to the shoulder of the opposite lane to go around a large rock. In addition to the large rocks, there are deep gullies in the roads caused from water draining during the rainy season. It can take a very long to travel a short distance because of the obstacles one must avoid.

I was seated next to a young man who was translating a conversation back and forth between our guide and me.

After we had swerved left and right, waited long periods for other vehicles to pass, and been bounced mercilessly along the roads for twenty minutes, without covering much more than a mile or two, I leaned toward our guide and said sarcastically, "Wow, nice roads."

Our translator sat silent.

"Aren't you going to translate what I said?" I asked.

"I can't," he said.

"Why not?"

"Because what you said was sarcastic, and the African people do not understand sarcasm. If I tell him you said the roads are nice, he will believe you. If I tell him you don't like the roads, it sounds critical."

"They don't ever speak sarcastically?" I asked.

"No, they don't have a word for sarcasm. They have no understanding of saying something and meaning its opposite," he said. "To them you say only what you mean."

"A sarcastic person has a superiority complex that can be cured only by the honesty of humility."

—LAWRENCE G. LOVASIK

Perhaps there is no connection between the upbeat demeanor of the people there and a lack of sarcasm. But maybe there is a peace that comes from knowing that when someone says something, he or she means it.

Incidentally, and this I believe correlates directly to their overall happiness, people in Africa consider it rude to complain to others. They think that taking your burden and placing it on another's shoulders does not lessen your unhappiness but adds it to the listener.

Criticism and sarcasm are two of the most insidious forms of complaining. Watch how often you criticize or make a sarcastic remark, and when you do, switch your bracelet.

CHAPTER 8

HONK IF YOU'RE HAPPY

The present moment is filled with joy and happiness.
If you are attentive, you will see it.

—THICH NHAT HANH

The Conscious Competence stage is what many have called the "I'm not going to move my bracelet" stage. You begin to say something, and realizing you are about to complain, gossip, criticize, or express sarcasm, you catch yourself, concluding, ". . . and I'm not going to move my bracelet." You then restate your comment or let it pass.

Many have found it helpful during the twenty-one-day challenge to get a "Complaint Free buddy." Consider posting a request on our Facebook fan page (www.facebook.com/A ComplaintFreeWorld) to find someone to share your experience and keep you motivated. Better yet, consider enlisting a friend or family member.

Note: A Complaint Free buddy is *not* a person to watch

> **VOICES**
>
> *I have been working on going complaint free and it is rubbing off on my family.*
>
> *My daughter Rose is a sixth grader with all the typical drama of adolescent girls.*
>
> *One of her "friends" wrote her a note stating that Rose was a terrible friend and listed a lot of reasons. It also stated that all the other girls in their clique feel the same way.*
>
> *When Rose told me this story I was really nervous because this is a big deal in the life of a sixth grader. I asked her what she did.*
>
> *Rose said she told the girl, "I'm going to pretend I never got that letter. From now on let's only say nice things to each other. I really like your shoes."*
>
> *The other girl was so surprised that she just started laughing.*
>
> *I'm so proud of my girl and I really think my bracelet and my explaining to Rose how I am not complaining has paid off.*
>
> —RACHEL KAMINER,
> WHITE PLAINS, NEW YORK

you like a hawk so as to point out when you complain. This is a person you can share your successes with and who will encourage you to continue when you have to start over at Day 1.

Find someone who can help you reframe the situations in your life in a positive manner; someone who will be on "blessing patrol," helping you seek out the potential good in whatever situation you are facing. You need a cheerleader, someone to encourage you when you're tempted to quit, a person who wants you to make it.

As I mentioned in Chapter 1, one of the most common side effects of becoming Complaint Free is an increased feeling of happiness. As you cease griping about the problems in your life and begin to talk about what is going well, your mind cannot help but respond to this new focus.

About twelve years ago, I met a man who helped someone he loved dearly reframe what seemed to be a negative, even tragic situation. Of all the stories I presented in the original version of this book, this is by far the most popular. It has been reprinted and distributed to several million people because the message in this true story is so simple and yet so profound.

> "Happiness is the only good. The time to be happy is now. The place to be happy is here."
>
> —ROBERT G. INGERSOL

It all started with a little sign.

The sign was made from a tattered piece of cardboard stapled to what looked like one of those sticks given away at hardware stores to stir paint. As I was about to cross the causeway over the Waccamaw River, just outside Conway, South Carolina, I noticed it one day. There, along the side of the road, shoved into the ground amid the litter and the fire-ant beds, it said simply,

Honk If You're Happy!

I shook my head at the naïveté of the sign's creator and continued driving—my horn silent.

"What a bunch of fluff!" I snorted to myself. "Happy? What is happiness?" I'd never truly known happiness. I'd known pleasure. But even in my moments of greatest pleasure and fulfillment, I found myself wondering when something bad was going to happen to bring me back to reality. "Happy is a scam. Life is painful and challenging, and if things are going well, there is something around the next corner that is going to snap you out of the happy fantasy really fast. Maybe you're happy after you die," I thought, but I wasn't even sure about that.

On a Sunday a couple of weeks later, my daughter Lia, then age two, and I were riding in the car down Highway 544 toward Surfside Beach to see some friends. We were singing along to a cassette labeled "Favorite Kids' Songs," laughing and enjoying our time together. As we neared the causeway to cross the Waccamaw River, I saw the sign again and, without thinking, tapped my horn.

"What?" asked Lia, wondering if perhaps there was something in the road.

"There's this sign on the side of the road that says HONK IF YOU'RE HAPPY," I said. "I felt happy so I honked."

The sign made perfect sense to Lia. Children don't have concepts of time, taxing responsibilities, disappointment, betrayal, or any of the other constraints or wounds that adults carry. To her, life is in the moment, and the moment is meant for happiness. When the next moment arrives, it too is meant for happiness. Honk and celebrate this happy moment.

Later that day, as we made our way home and passed the sign again, Lia shrieked, "Honk the horn, Daddy, honk the horn!" By this time, my perspective had shifted from earlier that day, when I'd been looking forward to time with friends, to thinking of the many pressing and stressful things that awaited me at work the next day. My mood was anything but happy, but I still tapped the horn to appease her.

What happened next, I'll never forget. Deep inside and just for a moment, I felt a little happier than I had just seconds before—as if honking the horn made me happier. Perhaps it was some sort of Pavlovian response. Maybe hearing the horn caused me to conjure up some of the good feelings I had when I'd honked that morning.

> "No man is happy who does not think himself so."
>
> —PUBLILIUS SYRUS

From that point on, we could not pass that particular

stretch of highway without Lia reminding me to honk. I noticed that each time I did, my emotional thermostat rose. If on a one-to-ten scale I was feeling an emotional two, when I honked the horn, my happiness grew to a six or seven. I noticed this happened each time we passed the sign and I honked the horn. I began to honk as I passed the sign even when I was alone in the car.

The positive feeling I had when I honked at the sign began to extend. I found myself looking forward to that particular section of road, and even before I reached the sign, I noticed I began to feel happier inside. In time, when I turned onto Highway 544, I noticed that my happiness set point would immediately begin to rise. That entire 13.4-mile stretch began to become a place of emotional rejuvenation for me.

> "With all its sham, drudgery and broken dreams, it is still a beautiful world. Be cheerful. Strive to be happy."
>
> —MAX EHRMANN, "DESIDERATA"

The sign was on the shoulder of the highway, next to some woods that separated nearby homes from the causeway. In time, I found myself wondering who put the sign up and for what purpose.

At that time in my life, I was selling insurance to people in their homes. One afternoon, I had an appointment to meet with a family who lived about a mile north of Highway 544, but when I arrived, the mother told me that her husband had forgotten our meeting and we would need to reschedule. For a moment I felt dejected, but as I was driving out of the housing development, I realized that I was on the backside of the woods that bordered the highway. As I drove along the road, I estimated where I was in relation to the HONK IF YOU'RE HAPPY sign, and when I felt I was close, I stopped at the nearest home.

The house was a one-story gray manufactured home with dark red trim. As I climbed the cinnamon stairs to the front deck, I noticed that the home was simple but well cared for.

I began to prepare what I would say if someone answered the door. I considered "Hi, I saw a cardboard sign on the highway on the other side of those woods and was wondering if you know anything about it." Or maybe "Excuse me, but are you the 'Honk If You're Happy' people?"

I felt awkward, but I wanted to know more about the sign that had had such an impact on my thinking and my life. After I rang the doorbell, I didn't get a chance to say any of the opening lines I had rehearsed.

"Come in!" a man said with a broad, warm smile.

Now I really felt awkward. I thought, "He must be expecting someone else and thinks I'm that person." I entered the

> "I have learned from experience that the greater part of our happiness or misery depends on our dispositions and not on our circumstances."
>
> —MARTHA WASHINGTON

home and he warmly shook my hand. I explained that I had driven the highway near his home for more than a year and had seen a sign that read HONK IF YOU'RE HAPPY. By my estimation, his house was the one closest to the sign, and I wondered if he knew anything about it. He smiled and told me he had put the sign up more than a year ago. Further, he told me that I was not the first person to stop in and inquire about it.

As I heard a couple of horn blasts from a car in the near distance, he said, "I'm a coach at the local high school. My wife and I enjoy living here near the beach and we love the people. We've been happy together for many years." His clear blue eyes seemed to penetrate mine. "A while back," he said, "my wife got sick. The doctors told her there was nothing they could do. They told her to get her affairs in order and said she had four months to live—six months at the outside."

I was uncomfortable with the brief silence that followed, but he wasn't. "First we were in shock," he said. "Then we got angry. Then we held each other and cried for what seemed like days. Finally we accepted that her life would be ending soon. She prepared herself for death. We moved a hospital bed into our room, and she lay there in the dark. We were both miserable."

"One day I was sitting on the deck while she tried to sleep," he continued. "She was in so much pain; it was hard for her to doze off. I was drowning in despair. My heart ached. And yet as I sat there, I could hear the cars crossing the causeway to go to the beach." His eyes drifted up to the corner of the room for a moment. Then, as if remembering he was talking to someone, he shook his head and picked up the story. "Did you know that the Grand Strand—what people call the sixty miles of beach along South Carolina's coast—is one of the top tourist destinations in the United States?"

"Um . . . yes, I do know that," I said. "More than thirteen million tourists a year come to vacation here."

"That's right," he said. "And have you ever been happier than when going on vacation? You plan, you save, and then you go off to enjoy some time with your family or your girlfriend. It's great."

A long honk from a passing car punctuated his point.

The coach thought for a moment and then continued, "It hit me as I sat there on the deck that although my wife was dying, happiness didn't have to die with her. In fact, happiness was all around us. It was in the cars that passed just a few hundred feet from our house every day. So I put up the sign. I didn't have any expectations for it; I just wanted the people in their cars not to take this moment for granted. This special, never-again-to-be-repeated moment with the ones they care for most should be savored, and they should be *aware* of their happiness in the moment."

Several honks sounded from different horns in rapid succession. "My wife began to hear the honks," he said, "just a few here and there at first. She asked me if I knew anything about it, and I told her about the sign. In time, the numbers of cars honking began to grow, and they became like medicine for her. As she lay there, she heard the horns and found great comfort in knowing that she was not isolated in a dark room dying. She was part of the happiness of the world. It was literally all around her."

I sat in silence for a moment, trying to take in what the coach had shared. What a touching and inspiring story.

"Would you like to meet her?" he asked.

"Uh, yes," I said with some surprise. We'd spoken for so long about his wife that I'd begun to think of her more as a character in a rich and wonderful story than as a real person. As we walked down the hall to their room, I braced myself so as not to appear shocked by the sick and dying person who awaited me. But as I entered, I found a smiling woman who seemed to be playing sick, rather than someone genuinely near death's door.

Another honk sounded, and she threw a playful smile at her husband. "There goes the Harris family," she said. "It's

> "When one door of happiness closes, another opens; but often we look so long at the closed door that we do not see the one which has opened for us."
>
> —HELEN KELLER

good to hear from them again. I've missed them." He returned her smile.

After we were introduced, she explained that her life was now as rich as ever. Hundreds of times a day and throughout the night, she heard the chirps, trumpets, bleets, blasts, and roars of horns telling her that there is happiness in her world. "They have no idea I'm lying here listening," she said, "but I know them. I've gotten to where I know them by the sounds of their horns."

She blushed a little and then continued, "I've made up stories about them. I imagine the fun they're having at the beach or playing golf. If it's a rainy day, I imagine them at the aquarium or shopping. At night I imagine them visiting the amusement park or dancing under the stars. They are leading happy lives." Her voice trailed off as she began to fall asleep. "What happy lives . . . what happy, happy lives."

> "Man is fond of counting his troubles, but he does not count his joys. If he counted them up as he ought to, he would see that every lot has enough happiness provided for it."
>
> —FYODOR DOSTOYEVSKY

Other than the honks outside the window, the three of us sat in silence for a few moments.

Finally, I looked at the coach. He smiled at me, and we both rose and made our way out of the bedroom. In silence he walked me to the door, but as I was leaving, a question came to me.

"You said the doctors gave her six months to live, right?" I asked.

"That's right," he said with a smile that knew my next question.

"But you said she was sick in bed for several months before you put up the sign."

"Yep," he said.

"And I've driven by and seen the sign now for well over a year," I finished.

"Exactly," he said, patting me on the shoulder. And then he added, "Please come back and see us again soon."

The sign was up for another year, and then suddenly one day it was gone. "She must be dead," I thought sadly as I drove by. "At least she was happy in the end and beat the odds. Weren't her doctors surprised."

A few days later I was driving along 544 toward the beach, and for the first time, I felt sadness rather than happiness as I approached the causeway. I checked again, wondering if the wind or rain had simply ruined the fragile little sign. But it was indeed gone. I felt dark inside.

I kept thinking about this woman who, in the midst of pain and death, had managed to find happiness. I thought how so many people who have all that she would have desired walk around miserable and complaining.

The following week, I again found myself traveling along Highway 544 toward the beach. As I approached the causeway, I noticed something wonderful. Where the little cardboard-and-stir-stick sign had once stood, there was now a new sign. It was six feet wide and four feet high, with a bright yellow background bordered with dazzling, flashing lights. On both sides of the new sign in large illuminated letters was the familiar HONK IF YOU'RE HAPPY!

With tears in my eyes, I leaned on my horn to let the coach and his bride know I was passing. "There goes Will," I imagined her saying with a wistful smile.

With the support of her loving husband, rather than focusing on what her reality was—a reality confirmed by medical experts—this wonderful woman had focused on the happiness all around her. And, in so doing, she had beaten the odds, embraced life, and touched millions of people.

Life is not about where you stand, it's about the direction in which you are heading. And this is determined by where you are looking.

From the moment we first draw breath, we are moving toward the grave. When we'll get there, none of us knows. The tragedy is not to die but to have never lived. To never have enjoyed where we are.

> "What a wonderful life I've had! I only wish I'd realized it sooner."
>
> —COLETTE

We tend to relegate happiness to "someday." When all of

our problems are resolved, we will be happy. Well, the only day you will no longer have problems is the day when you exhale for the final time. Until then, there will be challenges and struggles, so you might as well make the decision—yes, the decision—to be happy.

When I was in China a while back, I was having dinner with representatives from my Chinese publisher, Beijing Bookey. One of the dinner guests told me a very old Chinese story about a woman who was always unhappy.

As the legend goes, the woman had two sons. One sold umbrellas to make a living and the other sold salt.

Every morning, the woman rose and looked out of her window. If she saw sunshine, she would complain, "Oh, this is terrible, no one will buy my son's umbrellas."

If she looked out of her window and saw rain, she would complain, "This is bad! No one will come and buy salt from my son."

After years of being despondent, she finally consulted a Buddhist monk, asking what she could do to find happiness. His response was simple and profound. "Change the way you see things," he said. "If it is raining, give thanks that there will be demand for your son's umbrellas. If the sky is clear, celebrate that people will come and buy salt from your other son."

She took his advice and her life quickly changed. The only thing that changed was her perspective, but perspective is everything. Changing how we view the world causes us to see new things and to see old things anew. Chronic complaining keeps our focus on all things bad. Becoming Complaint Free lets us see that there is much to be happy about.

There is an admitted self-delusional quality to being happy. But there is also a self-delusional quality to being unhappy. Austrian-British philosopher Ludwig Wittgenstein said, "The world of those who are happy is different from the world of those who are not."

Life is an illusion. Our perspective is a delusion. Choose the delusion that brings you the only thing that matters—choose to be happy.

PART 4

UNCONSCIOUS COMPETENCE

CHAPTER 9

MASTERY

The sun was shining in my eyes, and I could barely see;
To do the necessary task that was allotted me.
Resentment of the vivid glow I started to complain.
When all at once upon the air I heard the blind man's cane.

—EARL MUSSELMAN

There are several species of fish known as blind cave fish. Most of them can be found in the United States, in the limestone cave regions of the Mississippi Delta. Blind cave fish grow up to five inches in length and have little or no pigmentation. In addition to their pale skin, all but one of the species have no eyes. Scientists conjecture that many years ago these fish's ancestors may have been trapped by shifts in the landmass or water channels and become cave-bound. Surrounded entirely by darkness and unable to see, the fish adapted to their surroundings. These species of fish now thrive in total darkness.

Over generations of producing offspring, blind cave fish ceased to produce pigmentation to protect their skin from the

VOICES

Four years ago my twenty-three-year-old son (my old-est), a police officer, suffered a bleed in his brain while driving. Without going into details it has been a long road, but one that my whole family has faced with trust in God and unconditional love.

Ben is recovering (all the docs said he wouldn't make it) and he accepts his disabilities with a peace that is such a lesson for us all. God's grace is active and growing in him.

He has mild aphasia, right side weakness, and some slower processing yet he continues to improve—all without complaining. Thus, the reason for the bracelets. If Ben can accept his cross without complaining, surely the rest of us can. I want people who have helped Ben in his recovery to all get a bracelet.

Thank you so much and continued GOOD LUCK with your mission. You have made an impact!

—NOREEN KEPPLE,

STONINGTON, CONNECTICUT

sun because it was no longer necessary. Similarly, over time, blind cave fish began to produce fry without eyes.

After you have gone the months it takes to become a Complaint Free person, you will find that you have changed. Just as over generations the bodies of blind cave fish stopped producing both pigmentation and eyes, you will find that your mind no longer produces a deluge of negativity. Because you are not articulating negative thoughts, the complaint factory in your mind closes down. You have shut off the spigot and the well has dried up. By changing your words, you have reshaped the way you think. It has now become Unconscious (you don't notice) for you to be Competent (not complain).

I conducted a seminar on becoming Complaint Free and wanted the audience to see how heavy and negative the energy in the room felt when everyone complained. I also wanted them to get some practice switching their bracelets with each complaint, so I invited everyone to pair off and take turns complaining and switching their bracelets.

> "No one ever complained their way to the top."
>
> —FRANK PERDUE

I noticed that one woman did not have anyone to be her partner, so I offered to do the assignment with her. She went first, complaining about her mother. After she switched her bracelet, she looked at me expectantly, indicating that it was my turn to complain. I stood in silence. I could not think of anything to complain about, and even when I did conjure something up, I realized it was very hard to form the words.

After many months of constantly watching every word I

said, my mind had changed. The factory had shut down the Complaint Department. Further, I had become so focused on catching and preventing myself from complaining, I felt as if lightning might strike me if I complained.

I was now Unconsciously Competent. I had become to complaining what blind cave fish have become to light. I had lost the capacity and the ability to complain. And what was most important was that I found that I was much happier for having made the effort to change.

This is why we offer a "Certificate of Happiness" rather than a "Complaint Free Certificate" whenever someone completes the twenty-one-day challenge. Because the experience of becoming happier has been so universal for those who have stayed with the challenge, we wanted to acknowledge the real transformation that takes place.

When you successfully complete your twenty-one days, go to our website, www.AComplaintFreeWorld.org, and download your certificate. It is a real accomplishment to have stayed with this, and your life will reflect your efforts in positive and exciting ways.

In the Unconscious Competence stage you are no longer an "ouch" looking for a hurt. Rather, your thoughts are now on what you want, and you are beginning to notice how what you desire manifests. Not only are you happier, but also the people around you seem happier. You are attracting upbeat people, and your positive nature is inspiring those around you to even higher mental and emotional levels. To paraphrase Gandhi, you have become the change you wish to see in your world. When something goes well for you, your immediate response is "Of course!" And when a challenge presents itself, you don't give it any energy by speaking about it to others; rather, you begin to look for a blessing, and in seeking, you find.

In the Unconscious Competence stage you will notice how uncomfortable you now feel when someone around you begins to complain. It's as if a very unpleasant odor has suddenly wafted into the room. Because you have spent so much time checking yourself against complaining, when you hear it coming from someone else it's like a clanging cymbal during a moment of sacred silence. Even though the person's griping isn't pleasant for you to hear, you won't feel compelled to correct the other person. Rather, you'll simply observe the complaining, and because you neither criticize nor complain, the person won't need to justify and perpetuate his or her behavior.

You will begin to feel gratitude for the smallest things. Even things you used to take for granted. For myself, I can remember thinking, "If I'd known the last time I brushed my hair was going to be the *last* time I'd brush my hair, I would have enjoyed it a whole lot more." (If you don't understand this comment, look at my photo on the book jacket.) As you settle into being Unconsciously Competent, your default mind-set will be one of appreciation. You will still have things you desire to obtain, and that's good. Now, with your newfound positive energy, you can hold an image in your mind of what you desire, knowing that it is, even now, moving toward you.

Your financial situation will probably improve as well. Money is, in and of itself, without value. Money is slips of paper and coins that *represent* value. As you begin to value yourself and your world more, you will vibrate at a level that attracts greater financial benefits. People will want to give to and provide for you things that you may have had to pay for in the past. I know of a man who receives a number of professional services free simply because the people providing these services like him and enjoy his energy. The same can happen for you.

> "Greatness does not approach him who is forever looking down."
>
> —THE HITOPADESA

Watch for the smallest act of kindness or generosity and be grateful. If someone holds a door open for you or offers to carry something for you, count it as an abundant blessing from the Universe, and in so doing, you will attract more.

Positive, happy people are simply more enjoyable to be around. Now that you are such a person, another way your finances may improve is through pay raises and increased job opportunities.

There are three things that dictate a person's level of income:

1. The demand for what you do
2. Your ability to do what you do
3. The difficulty in replacing you

A person can be trained to do most jobs, but someone who shines sunlight and joy on the office is worth his or her weight in gold.

I used to work for a radio station in Seattle, Washington. Our receptionist was named Martha. Martha had the widest, brightest, and most sincere smile I've ever seen. She was always complimentary, genuinely happy, and willing to do anything for anyone. You could feel her presence in the office, and everyone was more cheerful and productive when Martha was around.

A few years after I stopped working there, I went back to the station to visit some friends. Something was different. As I stood in the lobby, the whole energy and ambiance seemed to have changed. It was as if someone had painted the walls a darker color or perhaps the lighting had gone bad.

"Where's Martha?" I asked.

The sales manager sighed. "She was hired away for more than twice what we were paying her." She gazed slowly around the office and then added, frowning, "That company got a deal!"

Martha's happy, upbeat personality radiated out to everyone at the station, and her leaving had brought the overall level of happiness and productivity down. Salespeople said that client complaints increased both in number and vehemence without Martha there to sprinkle her sweetness onto customers when they called in.

One of the greatest gifts of becoming a Complaint Free person is the impact you will have on your family. Your children will tend not only to model your behavior but to adopt your outlook on life. They will entrain with you and begin to see things as you see them.

As a young boy, I watched my dad in the kitchen. Whenever he cooked, he always took a dish towel and draped it over his left shoulder; he called it, appropriately, his "left shoulder cooking towel." The towel hung there at ready should he need to remove something hot from the oven or to wipe his hands. Today, whenever I'm in the kitchen, you will always find me with my own "left shoulder cooking towel." I never place the towel on my right shoulder, always my left—just like Dad.

Perhaps my dad had seen his father do this and was mimicking him, who knows? All I know is that I picked this up from him, and it is so habitual that I never give it a thought. My father never sought to instill this idiosyncratic quirk in me, but his behavior did so.

As a parent, a grandparent, or an aunt or uncle, you, too, are modeling how impressionable youngsters will behave. Children become like the adults they see. You now know how destructive complaining is. Do you really want your children to become habitual complainers? Do you want them to adopt a gloomy worldview and to feel like disempowered victims?

After a recent speech, a woman approached me and asked, "How do I get my darn kids to stop griping about every little thing?" She then proceeded to complain to me in great detail about all the problems her children cause.

"Perhaps you might work at becoming Complaint Free yourself," I told the haggard mom, knowing that her children were just mirroring back her words and attitude.

She shot me an exasperated glance and said, "I wouldn't complain if it wasn't for my darn kids!"

Sigh.

I realize that before we adopted a Complaint Free lifestyle I was teaching Lia that being at the family dinner table was a time to gripe and gossip. I'm so grateful that now dinnertime is when we talk about what went well that day. This is what I want her to pass on to her, so she'll model it for her children, and they will model it for their children.

A person who does not complain tends to get what he or she desires more easily simply because people want to help an agreeable person more than they want to help someone who berates and harangues them. Now that you have become

Complaint Free, people are going to want to work with and for you, and you will achieve and receive more than you ever dreamed. Give it time, watch for it, it will happen.

I'm often asked, "But what about social causes that I'm passionate about? How can I help bring about positive change if I don't complain?" As we've discussed, all change begins with dissatisfaction. It begins when someone like you sees a gap between what is and what can be. Dissatisfaction is the beginning, but it cannot be the end.

If you complain about a situation, you may be able to draw others to you, but you won't be able to get much done, because your focus is on the problem and not the solution. Discern what needs to be done and then begin to speak in terms of what it will be like when the challenge no longer exists, when the gap is bridged, when the problem is solved; you will then excite people to join you in improving things.

"Complaining is a form of manipulation."

—GARY ZUKAV

Another benefit of not complaining is that you will find yourself angry and afraid less often. Anger is fear directed outward. And because you are no longer a fearful person, you will attract fewer angry and fearful people into your life.

In *The Seat of the Soul*, bestselling author Gary Zukav wrote, "Complaining is a form of manipulation." As we discussed in Chapter 4, complaints are often expressed to manipulate people and to have power over them.

I have a friend who was a minister in a small town. The sanctioning body for his religion sent a consultant to help him grow his congregation.

"Find something your flock is afraid of," the consultant said. "Use that to get them angry. They'll complain about the situation to others, and this will unify them and draw other people into the church."

This approach seemed to lack integrity to my friend, who saw the purpose of his ministry as serving those in need rather than riling up a mob. Calling one of his fellow ministers, he asked how this fear-mongering technique had worked in his church.

"It worked well," the other minister said. "It brought in a lot of new people. The problem is that they're a bunch of angry and fearful people who complain all the time—and now I'm stuck dealing with them."

The governing body of his denomination pushed my friend to follow the consultant's advice, but he refused. He resigned as senior minister of this church to become a hospital chaplain. He's living in integrity and is content.

If you want to see a great example of complaining used to garner power, watch the classic movie *The Music Man* starring Robert Preston. Preston plays the fast-talking and unscrupulous salesman Professor Harold Hill, who peddles band instruments. Arriving in River City, Iowa, he asks an old friend, played by Buddy Hackett, "What is something happening in River City that I can use to get the citizens upset?" Hackett tells him that the latest big news is that the town's first pool table just arrived.

Professor Hill seizes hold of this event. He sings a song that inflames the fears of the town over the delinquency and degeneracy that he associates with playing pool.

Hill's solution to the "moral corruption" and "mass hysteria" pool playing brings is for all the young men to join a band. And Professor Harold Hill, salesman extraordinaire, is there to save the day by selling everyone band instruments and uniforms. He complains to manipulate the townsfolk for his own profit.

Zukav is correct. Complaining is a manipulation of your energy, and now that you're a Complaint Free person, you'll notice when someone is using his or her negative words to manipulate you.

In my first job out of college I sold radio advertising. My boss taught me that when I wrote commercials I should always include the two things that motivate people to make a purchase.

"What are they?" I asked.

"Fear and desire," he said.

"If you want people to buy something," he explained, "make them afraid of what will happen if they don't. Then tell them how great things will be if they do."

I stared naively at him.

"If you can't convince them they'll get a great benefit from buying the product," he said, "at least scare them with what will happen if they don't—works every time!"

To paraphrase Professor Harold Hill, people will try and scare you into doing what they want by complaining—with a capital "C" and that rhymes with "T" and that stands for TROUBLE.

"But isn't complaining healthy?"

When I'm interviewed about the Complaint Free phenomenon, the media often want to pair me with some psychologist who espouses complaining as a tool to better physical and emotional health. When this happens, I remind them that I'm not out to change people. If people want to complain, more power to them! And, just to be clear, I am not advocating remaining silent when there is something that you can correct or improve. Don't hold back, don't hold it in, just make sure you are stating only the facts, to someone who can resolve the issue.

Don't cry out. Speak up.

As for complaining being health-inducing, remember my definition of complaining: "An *energetic* statement that focuses on the problem at hand rather than the resolution sought." Typically the energy in a complaint is a strong feeling of displeasure. "A strong feeling of displeasure" is the dictionary definition of anger. Complaining, therefore, is often an expression of anger.

There is a myth that expressing anger is healthy. It isn't.

> "Venting angry feelings increases aggressive inclinations, it does not decrease them."
>
> —DR. BRAD BUSHMAN

Dr. Brad Bushman, research professor at the Institute for Social Research, University of Michigan, has spent nearly twenty-five years researching anger. He states, "Our research clearly shows that venting angry feelings *increases* aggressive inclinations, it does not decrease them."

In an article posted on The Inquisitive Mind—Social Psychology for You (www.http://beta.in-mind.org) Bushman writes about catharsis theory—the psychological term for venting anger:

> *Catharsis theory holds that expressing anger produces a healthy release of emotion and is therefore good for the psyche. Catharsis theory, which can be traced back through Sigmund Freud to Aristotle, is elegant and appealing. Unfortunately, the facts and findings do not show that venting one's anger has positive value. It harms the self and others.*

Penn and Teller, the Las Vegas magicians and self-designated debunkers of popular belief, engaged Dr. Bushman to prove this point on their Showtime network program *Bulls**t!*

Bushman invited six college students to take part in a psychological experiment. Each student was placed in a small room, given a pen and a piece of paper, and asked to write an essay on a topic of his or her choosing. After approximately thirty minutes, John, Bushman's research assistant, collected the papers, telling the students that another student would grade their work.

In reality, there was no other student. John took a red marker and wrote, "F! Worst Essay I've Ever Read!" at the top of each student's paper. He then returned the essays to the students. In the video, you can see the anger in the student's faces for having received such a harshly critical review of their work.

John then brought in a pillow for each of half of the students and asked them to punch the pillow for several minutes to release the anger caused by the incident.

The other students, the control group, were given time to simply sit quietly and cool off.

John then returned to each of the students and told them they now had a chance to exact revenge on the student who had graded their paper. Remember, there *was* no other student; Bushman's research assistant John had written the failing grade and the critical comment on the essays, but the students in the experiment did not know this.

Entering the room in which each student sat, John carried with him a tray containing fiery hot sauce and a cup. He informed the students that they could choose how much hot sauce the fictitious "other student" would have to drink. After the students poured as much of the blistering liquid into the cups as they wished, the cups were weighed.

Here's the interesting part: the students who had hit the pillow and thereby ostensibly released their anger poured *much* more hot sauce into their cups.

Take this in for a moment. The popular catharsis or anger venting theory would have us believe that the students who pounded the pillow should have released their anger, blown off their steam, set free their demons, and a dozen other pithy little clichés. However, in reality, after having been invited to vent to their hearts' content, the students who punched a pillow held *more* anger and *more* resentment than the ones given a chance to sit quietly for a few moments.

Bushman states, "The results of our study show that people who vent their anger are about twice as aggressive as those who do nothing at all."

There was a second part to the study that even more dramatically demonstrates how venting *increases* rather than diminishes upset. The students were each given a sheet of paper containing a list of partial words and were asked to fill in missing letters for each. The list included:

CHO _ E

ATT _ C _

KI _ _

R _ P _

The students who had punched the pillow—who should have expelled their anger and, according to conventional wisdom, should have been more centered and peaceful—tended to complete the words as follows:

CHO**K**E

ATT**A**C**K**

KI**LL**

R**A**P**E**

Whereas the students who did not vent their frustration by punching a pillow completed the words this way:

CHO**S**E

ATT**A**C**H**

KI**T**E

R**O**P**E**

The students who punched the pillows took neutral partial words and added letters to create violent words. "Aggression becomes more likely after venting," reports Bushman. In short, this whole idea of getting anger out is a myth that has been accepted and popularized by counselors, psychologists, and the media for decades.

Let me be clear, there are people who are emotionally shut down and need to get in touch with their repressed feelings. This can be achieved through working with a qualified therapist or counselor. However, the idea that when a stressful or upsetting event occurs in the life of an otherwise emotionally healthy individual, he or she should punch something, yell, scream, throw things, or in any other way attempt to "get it out" is not substantiated by science.

> "When angry, count ten before you speak; if very angry, a hundred."
>
> —THOMAS JEFFERSON

Last week, I posted on the Complaint Free World Facebook fan page a statement that the idea of needing to get one's anger out is a myth and was immediately attacked by "experts." Venting anger has become an urban legend to which people desperately cling, and it self-perpetuates. To use bestselling author Malcolm Gladwell's term, the idea of venting anger has "become sticky," and so it cascades through our common belief structure.

Remember that when Copernicus published *De revolu-*

tionibus orbium coelestium (*On the Revolutions of the Celestial Spheres*) proposing that the earth rotated around the sun and not the other way around, he was attacked by experts of the day.

From the media and a bevy of so-called experts we hear that "getting out our anger" is necessary and we then follow their advice. In a paper titled "Catharsis, Aggression, and Persuasive Influence: Self-Fulfilling or Self-Defeating Prophecies?" that Dr. Brad Bushman coauthored with Ray F. Baumeister and Angela D. Stack, the researchers state, "Participants who read a procatharsis message claiming that aggressive action is a good way to relax and reduce anger subsequently expressed a greater desire to hit a punching bag."

In other words, when someone says venting our anger is necessary for mental health, we accept it as fact and look for opportunities to lash out, thinking it will make us healthier.

Wrong.

I realize that debating this notion is a hotly controversial thing for most people because the idea is so widely believed, but just as the fact that millions of people for thousands of years believing that the world was flat did not change the shape of our planet, the number of people, regardless of their scholastic degrees, believing in the theory of catharsis does not make it a viable approach to happier living. It is, according to Bushman, just the opposite.

Ask yourself, "If venting our anger made us happier, then wouldn't the biggest complainers also be the happiest people?"

Bushman states, "People who have problems dealing with their anger, if they go to see a therapist who has them vent their anger, they need to find a new therapist fast."

> If venting our anger made us happier, then wouldn't the biggest complainers also be the happiest people?

I'm not a psychologist. I don't even play one on television. My experience in this arena is based solely on my own life's metamorphosis after leaving behind constant kvetching, and the many people who have shared with me how much happier and healthier they have become by being Complaint Free. It seems to me that if complaining were a way to be healthy, then the people in the United States would be some of the healthiest people in the world. And yet with what many would call the greatest medical system on earth, the United States ranks *below* 93 percent of all other countries for heart disease deaths per capita each year. Dr. Bushman sees a link. He says, "Expressing anger is linked to higher risk of heart disease."

People in the United States also face challenges with high blood pressure, stroke, cancer, and other types of disease. "Dis-ease," get it?

Michael Cunningham, Ph.D., a psychologist at the University of Louisville, proposes that the human predilection for complaining probably evolved from our ancestors' way of crying out a warning when something threatened the tribe.

"We mammals are a squealing species," Dr. Cunningham says. "We talk about things that bother us as a way of getting help or seeking a posse to mount a counterattack." Rampant complaining is something

> "Those who do not complain are never pitied."
>
> —JANE AUSTEN

we no longer need but have yet to evolve beyond, because, as we've discussed, we derive psychological and social benefits when we complain.

When we complain, we are saying, "Something is wrong." When we complain often, we live in a perpetual state of "something is wrong," and this increases stress in our lives. Imagine if someone were constantly shadowing you saying things such as "Beware!" or "Watch out—something bad is going to happen!" or "Something bad that happened in the past means more bad things are coming." Would it not make your life more stressful if someone with you was repeatedly pointing out possible dangers and pitfalls?

Of course it would. And when you complain frequently, the person sounding the warning alarm is you yourself. You are raising your stress level by complaining. You are saying, "Something is wrong," and your body is responding with stress.

Our collective stress level reminds me of ROTC cadets at the university I attended. Whenever one of the cadets would walk past an upperclassman, he was required to "brace." "Bracing" meant the cadet would have to bring his elbows tightly into his sides, tuck in his chin, and tighten his entire body as if prepared for an attack. When our minds focus on what is wrong through complaining, our bodies respond. We brace physically and emotionally. Our muscles knot up, our heart rate increases, and our blood pressure goes up.

Does this sound healthy to you?

If you look at the biggest selling prescription drugs in the United States, according to a February 27, 2006, article on Forbes.com, seven of the of the top seven—that's right, all of them—are for illnesses that are exacerbated by stress. In 2010, $308 billion was spent on prescription drugs in the United States, most of them to combat stress-related conditions such as depression, heartburn, heart disease, asthma, and high cholesterol.

"Okay," you might be thinking, "I get that complaining increases stress and that heart disease, depression, and heartburn can be impacted by stress; but not asthma and high cholesterol."

A study by Andrew Steptoe, D.Sc., and colleagues from

University College London, studying the effects of stress on cholesterol, was detailed in *Health Psychology* (November 2005). In this experiment, Dr. Steptoe and his associates measured the cholesterol levels of a group of participants and then put them in stressful situations. After the stressful events, the researchers again tested each person's cholesterol level and found that it had increased considerably. Stress does increase cholesterol levels.

As for asthma, Heather Hatfield of WebMD says, "When our stress levels start to creep upward . . . asthma symptoms can kick into overdrive." Stress increases asthmatic flare-ups.

Talking to a psychologist or other counselor about stressful events in your life as a way of getting past them can be healthy. A good psychologist can give these incidents meaning and provide hope and constructive paradigms for better living in the future. However, venting to a friend, coworker, family member, or stranger can be an excuse for unbridled negativity that can draw more problems to us. Not to mention that this can ally us with negative people to whom we may become entrained.

There are times when we all need to process what's going on to get a better handle on our lives. Processing and complaining are *not* the same thing. Processing is sharing your *feelings* about something that has happened, not just rehashing the experience. If your boss yells at you, you may want to talk to your spouse about how it made you feel. You might say, "I felt surprised and sad when my boss yelled at me."

When processing an experience, make sure what you are saying is centered on your feelings and not on the story of what happened. Use feeling words such as

- Mad
- Sad
- Glad
- Happy
- Angry
- Afraid
- Joyous

Speak in the first person. "I feel afraid when you do that" owns the experience as yours and is Processing. However, saying, "I feel like you're a jerk when you do that" is simply name-calling with the insertion of "I feel" before the attack. Your feelings are the best indicator of how well you are living in integrity with your highest self, and discussing your feelings with another, without the backstory and drama of "he said/she said," can be healthy.

Even with a therapist it's important not to linger in the pain of any one experience for too long. In her paper "Complaints and Complaining: Functions, Antecedents, and Consequences," Dr. Robin Kowalski describes how she found that talking about problems *increased* their prevalence. Stating it succinctly, Kowalski wrote, "Symptoms increase with symptom reporting."

A good therapist knows how much time and energy should be devoted to the past and how to help you use what has happened to create a more desirable future. Therapy can be a wonderful tool to understand how your mind works and to begin to use your power to choose what you will think to create the life you desire.

In his play titled *Fiction*, one of Steven Dietz's characters remarks, "Writers don't like to write; they like to have written." Similarly, people rarely like to change, but they like to have changed. Difficult though it may have been, you have put forth the willingness, the time, and the effort to keep switching your bracelet, starting over again and again. You are a new person. You have changed, and this change will endure. Famous associate Supreme Court justice Oliver Wendell Holmes said, "A mind stretched by a new idea never shrinks back to its original dimensions." You've made it.

> "A mind stretched by a new idea never shrinks back to its original dimensions."
>
> **—OLIVER WENDELL HOLMES**

If you've read this chapter and not yet completed twenty-one consecutive days Complaint Free, let this serve as a promise of things to come, and as I've said repeatedly, stay with it!

You can do it.

There is an old saying, "When you're in a hole, stop digging." If your life up to this point has not been the way you want it to be, then stop digging the hole deeper by complaining.

In the next chapter, you'll hear from people who have completed twenty-one consecutive Complaint Free days and how their lives improved as a result.

CHAPTER 10

TWENTY-ONE-DAY CHAMPIONS

No price is too high to pay for the privilege of owning yourself.

–FRIEDRICH NIETZSCHE

This chapter is dedicated to and written by just a handful of the thousands of people who stuck it out and became what we like to call Twenty-One-Day Champions.

As you read their stories, notice common themes and also see if you can find aspects of yourself in their experiences.

CATHY PERRY

(Substitute Teacher)

My twenty-first complaint-free day was April 24—nearly ten months after I first began wearing my purple bracelet. Over the course of the challenge, I quit and restarted several times. It took weeks just to get through one day Complaint Free. It became much easier when my husband began wearing the bracelet; it helps to take up the challenge with another person where you can help support each other.

This challenge opened up my eyes to how much I complained. It was really a process of becoming aware of my thoughts and words. As soon as I realized what I was really focusing on, I was able to change my thinking about myself, about others, and about situations that I encountered every day. It's been a transformation from my daily litany of "I'm tired," "I don't get enough sleep," and "There's never enough time to get anything done" to sleeping well and feeling good. As my focus changed, it became easier to maintain a positive attitude, and I have continued to feel better as the effect of positive thinking snowballed in all areas of my life. I have more energy. I feel happier and much more relaxed. Relationships with my family have also improved; there are more compliments than complaints in our daily conversation. Our home is such a peaceful place now.

> "Our home is such a peaceful place now."
>
> —CATHY PERRY

The Complaint Free challenge is not an easy one. It takes time and conscious effort to make it through that first complaint-free day. But once your habits and your thinking start to change, it becomes easier. The key is to keep trying.

For me, this challenge was not just about stopping complaining; it's about turning the complaints into gratitude for the blessings that I have. I see the good instead of only seeing things to complain about.

DON PERRY

(Bridge Designer)

My wife started the Complaint Free challenge last July, and when she told me about it I was intrigued. I noticed a big difference in her, and so I started wearing one of the purple bracelets. I had it on for eight weeks before I completed one full Complaint Free day. It took me another five months to complete the twenty-one consecutive days of no complaining.

During this challenge I realized how much my complaining affected my mood and how pessimistic I had become about many things. I was surprised to learn how others reacted to my negativity. One day at work, my boss asked me about my purple bracelet. When I told him about the "no complaints" challenge, he was pleased and said, "When you go on a rant, Don, you're scary."

When I related this conversation to my family, they agreed that I "got scary" and oftentimes they wanted to leave the room when I "went off" while reading the paper or watching TV.

I now realize that much of my anger and complaining stemmed from my insecurity at my job. I would complain to anyone who would listen about the amount of work that I had or about the looming deadlines because I was just not sure that I could get it all done. And if I can't get it all done, does that mean that I'm not good enough to do the job? Consequently, I complained about it because I was fearful and angry. But now I realize that there's always going to be a lot of work to do, and all I can do is my best.

> "My boss now calls me 'Mr. Sunshine.'"
>
> —DON PERRY

This realization has helped me come to terms with the fact that I can't control everything that happens at work or in other parts of my life and that complaining won't help the situation. I found that the less I complain about it, the less I worry about it. Letting go of that obsessive worrying has helped me enjoy time at home more and simply become more relaxed.

The Complaint Free challenge has helped me to become happier with my work relationships and at home. My negative attitude was contagious in a poisonous way, but my new positive attitude is contagious in a healing way. The happiness it has given me has only spread. My boss now calls me "Mr. Sunshine."

MELANEE CARMELLA PACKARD

(Certified Life Coach)

When I first began dating my husband, over eleven years ago, we were a lot alike; we complained about *everything*: our childhoods, our former spouses, our jobs, our financial situations, our bodies, our friends; every conversation was about what was wrong with something in our lives. And that's how we lived each and every day.

About seven years ago I had this feeling that life wasn't supposed to be so bad and I wanted to find a way to enjoy it, rather than wallow in self-pity, anger, and hate. I decided to make some changes and began my path to living a life filled with joy and love. I called it my "quest for happiness." During that quest, I began to see life through new, optimistic eyes. It changed not only my life but also the lives of most of the people that surrounded me. The only person that appeared to be unaffected by this was my husband, Mike.

My husband just couldn't understand why I was trying to refrain from the negativity that used to fill every conversation we had, and this led to fewer and fewer conversations and interactions with each other, which began to cause friction in our marriage. I began to feel anxious and resentful toward him for always being negative. I had even nicknamed him

"Negative Nelly," and whenever he was around I would expect him to complain and be negative. It got so bad that our two daughters and I would feel disappointment and anxiety whenever we heard the garage door open, signaling that he was home. I was seriously contemplating divorce because I couldn't imagine living with his negativity anymore.

> "Our lives were changed forever and my marriage was saved!"
>
> —MELANEE CARMELLA PACKARD

There I was, claiming to be on a path to be "positive" and express only love, yet I was only expecting the worst from my husband! What was worse was that our children had learned, from me, to expect the worst from him, too. They were now projecting negativity toward him!

Then something *amazing* happened! I was led to read *A Complaint Free World*. I can't even remember what or who brought this book into my world, but what I *do* know is that I *had* to read it as soon as I possibly could. So I grabbed the kids and went to the library, where I checked out the only copy still on the shelf and began to read it immediately, and before I knew it, *WHAM* our lives were changed forever and my marriage was saved!

Your book and the lessons that lie within it taught me that whatever we expect of others is exactly what they give to us. It was an epiphany for me. I decided right then and right there, in that moment, to now expect only the best from my husband—*all the time!* I held a mini family meeting with our daughters and explained to them what I had learned, and they were excited to be a part of our "experiment."

That was over a year ago and we are still together and getting stronger. It's not perfect but there's definite progress; every day it gets easier and better. It took me ten months to go twenty-one consecutive days without complaining. My daughters and I still wear the purple bracelets as a constant reminder not to get caught up in the negative. Thanks to you, we now know that we deserve the best from everyone and we expect that now. And you know what? It's what we actually *get!*

It's been life-changing for all of us.

JILL WENDT

(College Professor)

I think of myself as a positive person; however, several summers ago I found myself thinking and acting miserable toward my husband and children. I was so grouchy I couldn't even stand myself!

I went online and decided that I needed to find something about complaining to read. I stumbled upon Will Bowen's book and quickly ordered it and downloaded the audio version to my iPod so I could listen while I drove.

It was just what I needed. The concepts presented started me on a personal journey in which I became skilled at first becoming aware of my words and then changing them, which in turn changed my behaviors and actions in a positive way. Eliminating needless complaints and gossip is quite challenging; however, when you have small successes along your journey, there is a sense of peace and connection to the greater good.

I teach at a Chandler-Gilbert Community College in Phoenix, Arizona, and was so moved by this concept that I incorporated it into my curriculum. I decided that I would not complete the challenge alone but would invite about 150 college students to do it with me!

A semester lasts only about four months, and I had only one student complete the twenty-one days in that time frame. However, something miraculous still happened! The students were assigned to write about their experiences and create websites demonstrating their learning. I was astounded to read about the students' journeys, which were unique and special to them. While not reaching the twenty-one days within the semester, they were nonetheless able to see and feel the positive impacts it had on them as well as those around them. This is just one of many things the students wrote:

Dear Professor Wendt,

I thoroughly enjoyed taking part in this experiment as well as taking your class! I learned a lot about human nature and how to better acknowledge the invisible fabrics that provide the rhyme and reason in our society. People are amazing as a whole and in groups. Being able to see the differences that comprise us all provides a great insight into where we came from, why and who we are.

If everyone on earth were to take part in the Complaint Free Challenge just imagine how many walls could dissolve between classes and cultures as a result!

Stemming off from that I would like it to be known that this was one of my favorite parts of your class! It seemed that the protective shields we all wear were brought down. Through the subject matter and your open-minded enthusiasm about your class I think we all tried to take a look at each other from another view.

Although I didn't make the twenty-one-day challenge within that semester I did make it the following one! It was a very unique and personal accomplishment. I continue to try to be aware of how words can hurt others as well as make us feel bad about ourselves. It is great when you notice your "un-said" words begin to shift to reflect a more positive and loving attitude."

I have continued to offer this challenge to my students. I have challenged over two thousand students now to embark on this journey, and many of them challenged their friends and loved ones as well.

> "If your intention is to seek a solution, then this process helps you train yourself to transform your thoughts, words, and actions accordingly."
>
> —JILL WENDT

While many haven't yet reached the twenty-one days of being Complaint Free, engaging in the process is where most of the learning and transformative changes took place. It is less about being perfect and never complaining and more about thinking about what you say, how you want to say it, and evaluating your intentions. If your intention is to seek a solution, then this process helps you train yourself to transform your thoughts, words, and actions accordingly. In addition to challenging my students, I have offered in-services to other college instructors to discuss ways in which this concept could be incorporated into their curriculum. Through these discussions I have shared the benefits I have experienced both inside and outside the classroom. This process has given me a more interpersonal approach to really connect to my students.

I really enjoy running into former students at the grocery store or the movie theater who still have their purple bracelets several years after they have taken my class. They always update me on their journey and what has transpired. They have shared stories of healed relationships, improved health, and how they see the world differently as a result of being solution-focused versus being the victim. I have seen firsthand how this movement can transform the classroom experience, transform individual lives, and build a more positive community. I am continually encouraged watching my students embrace this opportunity to make their own lives better as well as to better their communities.

HERB PIERSON

(Minister)

Will Bowen's book *A Complaint Free World* inspired me to take the pledge, wear the bracelet, and watch my life improve. Without telling anyone, I tried it myself.

The first few days were a breeze until I began to more fully understand and appreciate both the subtlety and the obviousness of complaining.

Dealing with the more obvious complaints was generally

easy; however, those deeper, subtler ones caught me off guard quite a bit. Nonetheless, in a matter of two weeks I was in full swing as my bracelet went from right to left wrist and back with ease.

About this time, I announced it to my wife and she joined the effort. Rather embarrassingly, she surpassed me inside of a month and was well on her way to modeling the awareness needed to improve our lives. Even as we both switched bracelets often, we could see growth and openness improving our lives. We were laughing more, sharing more, and generally using each challenge as a stepping-stone to moving forward. In this process, each of us repeatedly hit upon those dreaded days when we were only a week away from completing the twenty-one days only to watch ourselves slide back to Day 1 after a truly meaningless complaint.

> "Within weeks my congregation was buzzing about the improvements in their lives."
>
> —HERB PIERSON

We had now tested this program in our own life and marriage; it was time to ask the congregation to join us. As soon as I announced it, they were eager and we began that day. People took the pledge and purple bracelets adorned our sanctuary. We could see from afar when one would accuse another of complaining and watch their exasperation as they both switched bracelets.

I remember more than one Sunday when in the middle of my lesson someone would show or mime "switch your bracelet for what you just said."

With each such embarrassment, I took comfort in the knowledge that within weeks my congregation was buzzing about the improvements in their lives. Many folks exchanged tired old habits for smoother, more positive ways of dealing with life's everyday challenges.

We enjoyed the process so much that we made it a priority to share it with the community at large. We took the idea to our Chamber of Commerce and several of our town's larger institutions. We created posters and began a countywide campaign to awaken our collective awareness to a better and more positive way to interact. The title, *A Complaint Free World,* caught our listeners' ears and usually brought a smile to their faces. The bracelets were flying out the door and the positive comments were flowing back.

Within three weeks, with no budget and no staff, nine hundred had signed up! Our whole county has only sixty thousand citizens, so nine hundred signed commitments meant we were already at 1.5 percent of our entire population.

Now, several years later, I still receive eager e-mails and phone calls asking to join "the movement."

THERESE LÖVROS

(Teacher)

I live in Sweden and work with six-year-old children. I read *A Complaint Free World* about two and a half years ago. I'm a teacher and had a really hard time trying to find a way to correct my pupils without complaining.

Now I have found a way to talk with them and help them think about how they learn and how they behave. We talk about what kind of results they get when they do what they do and whether or not the result is what they want. If it isn't, we figure out together what to do instead to achieve their goals.

As a result of my efforts to get through to the pupils without complaining, I have learned how to talk with their parents, my coworkers, and my friends as well. This has made my relationships much better and I feel more positive and happy.

"I feel more positive and happy."

—THERESE LÖVROS

I have realized that I can't stop complaining in just one area of my life, I have to live it, and that has made me see wonderful new possibilities in all things where other people might see only problems.

ANITA WIXON

(Writer)

Honestly, when I entered my seventh month of working on becoming Complaint Free I was extremely frustrated and upset. I had only successfully made it six or seven days in a row without having to move my bracelet. The biggest obstacle that kept me switching wrists was the fact that when Will first talked about this exercise, one of the stipulations was "no sarcasm."

Ouch!

I was having a hard time finding a new way to be clever and humorous without being sarcastic! On top of that, my business dictated that I do a lot of driving. Although I see myself as an excellent driver, I discovered that the flip side of this belief is that I also tend to believe that everyone else is a terrible driver! It seemed like I could not drive to the store without switching wrists.

One winter day, I decided it was time for a break. I took a few months off and gave myself a permission to not pay attention to the whole complaining thing for a while. During my hiatus, I realized I had already changed more than I thought. I no longer had any desire to become involved in gossiping conversations or complain. I paid attention to what came out of my mouth and paused before speaking to make sure what I was saying would convey the most positive energy possible rather than being sarcastic.

It also became apparent to me that there were certain people in my life that all we had in common was the bond of complaining: with each other, about each other, about others, and about the weather. I began to distance myself from those people and started working on attracting more positive people into my life. Ironically, even my driving improved.

More determined than ever, I put the purple bracelet back on early one spring morning with the intention to accomplish twenty-one consecutive days without complaining. Soon I made it all the way to eighteen days. But old habits die hard: while I was on the way to an appointment (at church, of all places!), a little old lady pulled out in front of me. Before I knew what happened, I was slamming on my brakes, cursing her, and blaring my horn! As soon as I realized what I had done, I started laughing. I wanted to follow the person and thank her for reminding me I had a way to go.

> "My habit now is to seek the positive, speak the positive, and live the positive."
>
> —ANITA WIXON

I made my twenty-one days just fifteen days short of a year from the date I first put on one of the purple bracelets. Although I do not wear the bracelet any longer, I do keep some handy as a reminder of my experience in changing my thoughts. My habit now is to seek the positive, speak the positive, and live the positive. When I find myself off track, I gently nudge myself back on the positive energy path with kind words and the memory of switching that little purple bracelet from wrist to wrist.

BARBARA WAYMAN

(Public Relations)

I wasn't a big complainer, but I started to notice more complaints around me and feeling like a crankypants more than I really wanted to. Soon after this awareness I came across the Complaint Free book and bracelets on a table at a networking event. I was totally ready and primed for the challenge so I jumped right in.

It has been an awesome journey.

Not wanting to change my bracelet, I've carefully thought through statements before I say them. Now, instead of expressing a negative, I switch it around and state what outcome I want or just make a neutral, factual statement without any blame or negatively charged energy. There's so much I don't even feel the need to say out loud.

> "I feel more peace, moving through my day giving others the benefit of the doubt and bouncing back from minor irritations that before would have truly bugged me."
>
> —BARBARA WAYMAN

I've let go of venting, and as a result, I feel more peace,

moving through my day giving others the benefit of the doubt and bouncing back from minor irritations that before would have truly bugged me. I want to thank you, Will, for this powerful and yet simple program that has helped so many people live a more positive and productive life. I think of the space around me as a Complaint Free zone, and I honor it every day.

I feel more cheerful, lighter, open, and more loving since embarking on this journey.

MARTY POINTER

(Computer Technician)

Since I managed to get through twenty-one days without complaining, I think the greatest benefit I've noticed is it is easier to embrace people who don't share my values and to accept events I can't control. I don't have to work as hard now at letting things go. I find myself gently gravitating away from folks who seem to enjoy criticism and finding fault, toward those who look for the best. A great reward has been several blossoming friendships with kindred spirits I may never have known without completing the twenty-one-day challenge.

By finishing the twenty-one days, I've discovered goodness in myself that I never really believed was there. While no one behaves perfectly all the time—and I admit to an occasional relapse—I've found it so much easier to see the light within

myself after learning to see past what I perceive to be imper-
fections in people and circumstances.

As I write this, my ninety-three-year-old mother lies in
her bed at home waiting to
join her parents and many
other loved ones who've gone
on before her. She weighs
eighty pounds and hasn't
eaten for over a week. The
hospice nurse says she doesn't
know why my mama is still
here because all of her re-
serves are gone. She is so weak and helpless. This situation has
been very painful to me, and I was struggling to suppress my
complaints toward God, until I called on the many lessons I
learned while doing the challenge. One of these, I recalled, was
asking for help. So I asked God for help.

> "I find myself gently
> gravitating away from folks
> who seem to enjoy criticism
> and finding fault, toward
> those who look for the
> best."
>
> —MARTY POINTER

Yesterday I awoke with the insight that God gave my
mother a wonderful, strong body that has served her in good
health for ninety-three years. It has carried her to many destinations, borne and fed three babies, played musical instruments, crocheted afghans, spoken and written her thoughts,
and done her will in myriad ways. That body is still faithfully
trying to do its job of housing her spirit, even as it fails little by
little. I'm now able to praise God in gratitude for this marvel-

ous gift, and thankfully accept His plan for how the earthly part of her soul's journey ends.

While visiting with the hospice chaplain, I was able to get a personal glimpse of how the Complaint Free movement can change the world. The chaplain's eyes started shining as I explained the challenge to her, and before my explanation was even finished, she asked me for fifty bracelets to give to the hospice staff. She said that although hospice workers have passion for service to the dying, they are human with all the trimmings. She thinks they will embrace the opportunity to serve better by concentrating even more on putting out only positive energy.

Six months ago, I would never have imagined how twenty-one days of Complaint Free living would change my life, but it truly has and now affects the lives of others around me.

GARY HILD

(Executive Chef)

In my career as a professional chef, I feel I have to be critical, with high expectations of my staff and myself to assure that we consistently put out top quality, creative food and presentation for guests with ever more sophisticated and varied palates.

Over the thirty-plus years I've lived my work life in professional kitchens, I've progressed from the old European style of tough, top-down management to a more humane and effective coaching approach.

The Complaint Free process turned out to be an idea that worked in ways I couldn't have anticipated. Specifically, after "graduating" the twenty-one straight days without complaining, I was so much more aware of how I communicate with my staff. I choose my words much more carefully now and think of my role more as a teacher with excellent culinary skills, rather than as a boss or manager. This frees up energy on my part as well as others around me for more enjoyable and stress-free dialogue.

> "My thinking and conversations are more oriented toward thankfulness and solutions, which attracts more of the same."
>
> —GARY HILD

I believe the Complaint Free process goes hand in hand with the Law of Attraction. My thinking and conversations are more oriented toward thankfulness and solutions, which attracts more of the same.

Today I still wear my bracelet as a reminder and practice only one method of response to the daily workload: extreme gratefulness shared in the most positive way. If I'm tempted to criticize, I stop and strive to present what I have to say in more of a teaching or instructional way, and people seem to feel more appreciated and heard. This has changed my outlook on everything and I feel freedom from stress and worry, kind of a by-product of the whole process. I am very blessed and grateful.

MARTI LEE

(Yoga Teacher)

I was born in Cuba and raised in Brooklyn, New York. Most of my family has a great sense of humor; however, much of their humor is based on making fun of others and making sarcastic remarks about something that has gone wrong.

Practicing yoga led me to being kinder in my words and opinions. I noticed a shift in my energy. My love of yoga opened me up. I went deeper into spirituality. I began incorporating chanting mantras and meditation to my yoga practice.

The practice of not complaining sounded really intriguing to me. It also went along with my lifestyle. It goes with the idea that you attract to yourself what you talk about and think. I jumped in with both feet. I put the purple bracelet on and was pumped to start. I am a really upbeat person and thought going twenty-one days without complaining would be a breeze.

Then I became aware that I would complain about various things with my mom and my girlfriends. I made announcements to my students, family, and friends that I had started this practice to stop complaining for at least twenty-one days.

It surprised me that this announcement actually upset my son. He said that I was going to be a "drag." He said he was afraid that I was going to stop being funny.

It was touch and go for three full months. I seriously contemplated taking a vow of silence. My New York sarcasm was hard to tame.

I learned so much from this program. I wanted to share it with anyone who would listen. This is a modern practice that is also just as powerful as the ancient

> "When you stop complaining it takes your consciousness higher into being more grateful."
>
> —MARTI LEE

spiritual disciplines. When you stop complaining it takes your consciousness higher into being more grateful.

I saw immediately how my life was improving in all areas. For me it was the start of a journey, a simple strategy to apply in all conversations. Before you speak, ask, "Do I need to weed out anything that sounds like a complaint because the weeds in a conversation will eat away the nutrients of my loving words?"

Since my intention in all my interactions is to connect and grow, complaining had to be weeded out.

I did it! It took me three months, but I made it twenty-one days in a row without complaining.

And I'm still funny—at least my kids think so.

TOM ALYEA

(Business Consultant and Voluntary President

of A Complaint Free World)

As a fan of the old *I Love Lucy* shows, I used to love it when Ricky Ricardo walked through the door each day and shouted, "Hey, Lucy, I'm home." For the first years of my marriage I would do the same: "Hi, Mischa, I'm home." But at some point in my life it got to be a lot easier to say, "Hi, Mischa, I'm home, and my head, back, feet, or stomach hurts."

Complaining had become a way a life for me—a way to get attention, a way to just open a conversation. I always saw myself as such a positive, happy person. That was until I discovered the twenty-one-day challenge to stop complaining.

I was excited and told my wife that I was going to be the first to make the twenty-one days Complaint Free. She just smiled and said, "Twenty-one days? I'd like to see you go twenty-one minutes without complaining."

About six minutes later, I realized that this was going to be the challenge of a lifetime. My wife and I were sitting on the couch and all of a sudden I said, "Wow, it's really hot outside, and it sure is making my head hurt." She looked at me, looked at my bracelet, which I switched right then and there—twice because I complained two times in just one sentence.

The truth is that the silence in those six minutes was driving me nuts and I had to open a conversation with something. I wanted attention and thought complaining was the best way to get it.

So that was my first challenge: to learn how to start a conversation without a complaint. Once I had worked on that, then I moved on to other complaints. The kids' rooms are a mess. Tell me, does complaining about a teenager's room ever really get it cleaned any faster? The weather—well, what can I do about it? And the list went on and on as I realized just how negative my thoughts and words tended to be.

After spending five months working on the twenty-one-day challenge, I finally made it! Do I have fewer headaches? Yes, because I realized I didn't have too many of them in the first place. What I see now is a body that is healthy and whole and is working on healing all the time.

> "This has been the best thing to happen in my life, ever."
>
> —TOM ALYEA

Am I happier? You betcha! Dinners with the kids are a lot nicer when talk is less about complaining about dirty rooms and more about their hopes and dreams. Am I glad I persevered and made it the twenty-one days? Short of a wonderful marriage, and three kids whom I love and adore, this has been the best thing to happen in my life, ever.

UVA UVAM VIDENDO VARIA FIT

How many a man has dated a new era in his life
from the reading of a book.

–HENRY DAVID THOREAU

Y ou have entered into a new era in your life.

The concepts you have learned in this book have tweaked your consciousness and opened up new possibilities whether you fully realize it or not. Chances are you have not even begun to embrace all of the many ways your life will improve as a result of this process.

If you have spent your life focusing on clouds, soon you will begin to see the sunlight that shines brightly behind them. If you have been plagued by dissatisfaction, you will begin to find peace and joy. If you have seen only problems, you will begin to discover new possibilities. If your relationships have been discordant, you will begin to experience harmony.

You have planted a seed. It may seem to be just a small acorn, but in time it will grow into a majestic oak.

VOICES

Like thousands, I have already begun changing my focus. While waiting for my bracelet, I have started to wear a rubber band around my wrist. This has made me aware of what I'm doing. I've been doing this for about a week, and I am now rarely complaining.

The remarkable thing about this is how much happier I feel! Not to mention how much happier those around me must be (like my husband!). I have wanted to work on my complaining for a long time and the bracelet campaign has been the impetus for changing my behavior.

The bracelets and the mission behind them have come up in MANY conversations, so the mission has a HUGE ripple effect where MANY people are at least thinking about how often they complain and perhaps deciding to behave differently. This movement may have a very far-reaching effect as more and more people hear of the idea.

The reach of this mission is far greater than those who actually get the bracelets!

Awesome to think about!

—JEANNE REILLY,

ROCKVILLE, MARYLAND

Your life is transforming.

Let me say one more time that you can succeed at becoming Complaint Free if you will just stay with it. People are creatures of habit. It takes time to replace old habits with new ones. But a habit is created with single actions like single brushstrokes on what will one day become an enormous ball of paint.

When I was a child, one of my favorite books my mother would read to me was about a baker, a miserly shopkeeper, and the mysterious stranger who enters their village. In this story, the stranger approaches the townsfolk asking for food and shelter for the night. When he asks the miserly shopkeeper and his wife if they will help him, the couple dismissively refuses to provide assistance.

The stranger then walks into the town's only bakery. The baker is penniless and nearly out of baking supplies. Nonetheless, he invites the man in and shares a meager meal with him. Then the baker offers the man his own austere bed in which to sleep. The next morning the stranger awakens, thanks the baker, and tells him, "Whatever you do first this morning, that you will continue to do all day."

The baker is unsure as to the meaning of the stranger's comment and gives it little thought. He decides to bake his guest a cake to take with him. Surveying the last of his supplies, he finds two eggs, a cup of flour, a little sugar, and some spices. He begins to bake, and to his surprise discovers that the more supplies he uses, the more supplies there are. As he draws out the last two eggs, he notices four more in their place. When he tips the flour sack to shake out the last handful, the sack is full when he sets it down. Overjoyed with his good fortune, the baker throws himself into baking all manner of delicacies, and soon the town square is filled with the delicious aroma of baked breads, cookies, cakes, and pies. Customers line up around the block to purchase his confections.

That evening, tired, happy, and his cash register overflowing, the baker is approached by the miserly shopkeeper. "How did you get so many customers today?" the shopkeeper demands. "It looked like everyone in town bought baked goods from you, some more than once." The baker shares the story of the stranger he had helped as well as the man's enigmatic blessing prior to departing.

The shopkeeper and his wife run out of the bakery and down the road leading from town, in search of the mysterious stranger. At last they find the man they refused to help the night before. "Gentle sir," they say, "please, forgive our rudeness last night. We must have been out of our heads not to help you. Please, return with us to our home and allow us the honor of sharing our hospitality with you." Without a word, the man turns around and joins the couple on the road back into town.

When they arrive at the shopkeeper's home, the traveler is

fed a sumptuous meal with fine wine and a decadent dessert. The stranger is then offered a luxurious room for the night with a bed made from thick, cozy goose down.

The next morning, as the visitor prepares to leave, the shopkeeper and his wife bounce up and down on their heels expectantly waiting for him to cast his magic spell over them. Sure enough, the stranger thanks his hosts and says, "Whatever you do first this morning, that you will continue to do all day."

Having received the blessing, the shopkeeper's wife rushes the stranger out the door. She and her husband put on their cloaks and dash to their store. Expecting a large number of customers, the shopkeeper grabs a broom and begins to sweep the floor in preparation for the onslaught of traffic. Wanting to make sure they have enough change for the purchases certain to happen that day, his wife begins to count the money in the till.

The shopkeeper swept and his wife counted. She counted and he swept. Try as they might, they could not stop sweeping and counting until the day was over. When someone did enter their store, they were so compelled to continue sweeping and counting that they were unable to stop to sell anything.

Both the baker and the shopkeeper had received the same blessing. The baker began his day in a positive and generous way and received great reward. The shopkeeper began his day in a negative and self-serving way and derived nothing. The blessing was neutral.

Your ability to create your life is neutral. Use it however you wish; you will reap what you sow. This story reminds us that when we do things for others out of compassionate generosity rather than selfishness, we experience great rewards.

An important secondary moral to this tale is to begin each day as we wish the remainder of the day to unfold. If you have not been able to go even one full day without complaining, see how long you can go without complaining after rising in the morning. If you will attempt to go just a little longer each morning without speaking that first complaint, you will find yourself progressing much more quickly and easily toward your twenty-one-day goal.

GOGI:
Garbage Out of your mouth,
Garbage Into your life!

There is a term in computer programming usually expressed as an acronym: GIGO, which means "Garbage In—Garbage Out." If a computer does not perform properly, it is generally because there is something that has been input into the computer that is problematic. The garbage going in has generated garbage coming out. The computer is neutral.

Your life is like the computer—neutral. However, rather than Garbage In—Garbage Out, you will experience Garbage Out—Garbage In. What you speak sends out vibrations and calls more of what you say back to you. When you complain, you are sending out garbage and should therefore not be surprised when garbage shows up on your doorstep. Garbage Out of your mouth, Garbage Into your life!

What you articulate, you demonstrate. Talk about negative and unhappy experiences, and you will receive more negative and unhappy experiences to talk about. Talk about things you appreciate, and you will draw more positive things to you. You have a habitual pattern of speaking that demonstrates what you are thinking, and this is creating your reality. Whether you realize it or not, you plot your course each day and then follow that course.

If we want to improve the world, it must first come from our healing the discord within our own souls. Changing our words will ultimately change our thoughts, and this will in turn change our world.

> "To produce a different future I must be a different person."
>
> —JOHN P. HANLEY

When we cease complaining, we remove the outlet for our negative thoughts, our minds shift, and we become happier. Having no place for the negative thoughts to be expressed, the mind ceases production of them. When your mouth stops expressing negative thoughts as complaints, you will discover new, happier thoughts currently hidden behind the fog of negativity that shrouds your thinking.

Once you have completed twenty-one consecutive days

Complaint Free, you will move from being a person who is addicted to complaining to being one who is in recovery from a complaining addiction. Recovering alcoholics say that no matter how long they've been sober, if they spend enough time around booze, they are going to drink. If people around you are complaining, remain vigilant not to join in. You may have to extricate yourself from negative relationships. If they are at your place of work, change departments or change jobs—the Universe will support you along your positive new path. If they are with friends, you may realize that you have evolved beyond the present relationship. Even if the negative relationships are with family members, it may be best to limit your time with those people.

Don't allow people who are negative to rob you of the life you desire. It takes twenty-one days to form a habit. You can reverse the Complaint Free habit with twenty-one days of your old behavior, so be aware of those around you, because you may be tempted to follow their lead. Take care of yourself and beware of toxic, complaining people. If you are not mindful, you could entrain with them and sink back into the mire of negativity.

Love others. The best definition of "love" I've ever found comes from Dr. Denis Waitley: "Love is unconditional acceptance and looking for the good." As we accept other people and situations and look for the good in them, we will experience less to complain about. Loving others means not trying to get them to stop complaining. Rather, it's sweeping off your own doorstep, knowing that it is the surest way to clean the entire world.

As you become Complaint Free, it's not what you say but your energy behind your words that is important. When something good happens, no matter how small, say, "Of course!" knowing that you are a magnet for beneficence. You might even put a knowing smile on your face to anchor the experience.

Did you find a parking place right in front of the store you're visiting on a rainy day? Say, "Just my luck!"

Did you forget to put money in the parking meter only to return and find no ticket under your windshield wiper? Affirm, "This always happens to me."

As you begin to speak this way, it may feel silly, but every time you use affirmative words to describe your experiences you are putting solid bricks into the foundation of a better life.

> "It is a waste of time to be angry about my disability. One has to get on with life and I haven't done badly. People won't have time for you if you are always angry or complaining."
>
> —STEPHEN HAWKING

Because of you and the tens of millions of other people who are, right now, switching their bracelets and continuing along the Complaint Free path, I have hope that the prevailing attitude of the world will shift.

I shared this hope with someone the other day who said, "Sounds like false hope to me."

False hope? Let me share a story about "false hope."

It began at 1:10 A.M. on July 11, 2001. I was sound asleep, so it took several minutes for me to realize that the phone by my bed was ringing. Fumbling the receiver as I brought it to my ear, I croaked a weak "Hello?"

"Will? It's Dave," my younger brother said. "Mom has had a heart attack and it doesn't look good. You better come."

I got out of bed, packed a suitcase, and drove forty miles to the Kansas City airport. I tried to nap on the plane but found I was too worried. When my plane arrived at the airport in Columbia, South Carolina, Dave picked me up.

Before going to the hospital, we stopped at a local diner for a quick lunch and Dave filled in the details. "Last night at about eight-thirty, she began to have pain in her chest and back," he said. "She took some over-the-counter pain medications, but it didn't help. They took her to the hospital, but when they realized she was having a severe heart attack, the doctors had her flown via helicopter to the hospital here in Columbia that specializes in heart problems. She's awake but in a lot of pain."

Fifteen minutes later, Dave and I entered the Cardiac Critical Care Unit and found the room where our mother was sitting up with the aid of our oldest brother, Chuck. She was alert but was gasping slowly for breath. The medical staff gave us a few moments with her and then asked us to give her time to rest.

Our mother fell into a deep sleep and she did not wake up. Echocardiograms showed that she had suffered a major heart attack. "It's as if a large portion of her heart has been blown out," said one doctor.

In case she regained consciousness, I chose to spend several of the subsequent nights sleeping in the waiting room. Many times each night I would go in and check on her, but she remained comatose, her breathing made possible by a ventilator.

Even if you have no medical training, when you spend enough time with someone who is hooked up to a monitor that updates and reports vital signs, you can begin to discern when certain indicators are improving. Early one morning I noticed that my mom's blood oxygen level was rising and enthusiastically expressed this to her nurse.

"Don't get false hope," the nurse said with a compassionate smile.

That afternoon, I left to take a shower and to change clothes. When I returned to the hospital, I ran into an old college fraternity brother who is now a senior cardiologist on staff at this hospital. I asked him to review my mother's charts and tell me, honestly, her prognosis.

I returned with a cup of coffee an hour later to find my friend sitting in the waiting area. His face was grim.

"It's not good," he said. "Her heart has suffered major damage. I know you don't want to hear this, but it seems that the machines are the only thing keeping her alive."

I slumped in my chair and he placed a caring hand on my shoulder. As tears slipped down my cheeks, I stammered questions. "But can't *anything* be done? And what about her vital signs? Some of them seem to be improving. Isn't that good? Doesn't that indicate that she might recover?"

He squeezed my shoulder, took a deep breath, and said, "Will, yes, some of her vitals seem to have improved—slightly—but it doesn't change the fact that she has had a major heart attack. A little improvement isn't enough."

My friend let his words sink in and then said, "Earlier you asked me what I thought her chances of recovery were. Well, I'd say only about fifteen percent."

"Okay," I said. "That's fifteen percent, which is better than nothing, right?"

His compassionate gaze became stern. "Will, holding on to false hope is only going to make it more painful when she doesn't recover. I know you don't want to, but you have to face facts."

I tried to thank him, but I had no words. We exchanged a brief hug and he went back to his duties. I sat quietly and began to grieve my mother's passing.

That night I lay on the floor of the waiting room and thought of all the wonderful times I had enjoyed with my mom. I thought of all the things yet to come that she would not get to see in the lives of her grandchildren. I thought of all the things yet unsaid. My soul felt like a chalkboard that had been raked by the fingernails of her sudden illness.

Unable to sleep, I walked in sock feet down to my mother's room to check on her. The repeated *shhhrrrr . . . fuhhhh* sound of the ventilator gave the room an industrial feeling. I sat in the chair next to my mother's bed and held her hand. As I gazed at the monitor, I saw that many, not just some but most, of her vital signs had improved from earlier that day. I pointed this out to the nurse who came in to change the bag of glucose that dripped into my mother's veins.

Looking up at the monitor, the nurse said, "Her stats are better." She then added, "But don't get false hope."

A shudder of anger came over me. I dropped my mother's hand, turned, and jogged briskly down the hallway back to the waiting room. Turning on the lights, I tore a page from my journal. I found a pen and began to write in large letters on the page. Again and again I retraced pen strokes in an effort to make the letters as bold as possible. I then walked back to my mother's room and, using a piece of medical tape, pasted a sign on her monitor that read:

There is no such thing as false hope!

The word "hope" is defined as "a wish coupled with a confident expectation of its fulfillment." So long as you hold a confident expectation of what you desire coming to pass, it can never be false.

"False hope" is an oxymoron.

My mother did pass away. But not for another ten years. She lived another decade in relatively good health. New arteries actually grew around the damaged areas of her heart, returning her blood flow to near normal levels. My family and I had held a wish that she would recover coupled with a confidant expectation of her doing so, and there is nothing more powerful.

Join me in the hope that humanity will continue to shift away from fear and negativity toward faith and optimism. Your becoming a Complaint Free person is the most important step toward that hope becoming fulfilled. As one person changes, that person affects a great many people.

In Larry McMurtry's novel *Lonesome Dove*, one of the lead characters, a pseudo-intellectual cowboy named Gus McCrae, carves a Latin motto into the bottom of a sign he created for his livery business. The motto reads: UVA UVAM VIVENDO VARIA FIT.

McMurtry does not explain the motto and actually misspells it, I presume as a way of showing the cowboy's poor grasp of Latin. The correct spelling is *Uva Uvam Videndo Varia Fit*, which means that one grape changes color when it sees another. Put another way: one grape ripens another.

In a vineyard, one grape will begin to ripen, and in so doing it will send out a vibration, an enzyme, a fragrance, or an energy field of some kind, which is picked up by the other grapes. This one grape signals the other grapes that it is time to change; it is time to ripen. As you become a person who speaks only the highest for yourself and others, simply by being who you are you will signal everyone that it is time for a change. Without even trying, you will raise the consciousness of those around you. They will entrain with you.

Entrainment is a powerful principle. I think this is why human beings like to hug one another. When we hug, even for just a brief second, our hearts entrain and we remind ourselves that there is only one life on this planet, a life we all share.

If we don't choose how we live our version of this one life with intention, we will live it by default, following along with others. Rather than knowing that we lead the flock, we allow the flock to lead us. People follow along after others without even realizing they are doing so.

When my father was a young man, he managed a motel

owned by my grandfather. The motel was directly across the street from a used car lot, and my dad worked out an arrangement with the owner of the car dealership. On evenings when the motel's business was slow, my father would go over and move a dozen or so cars from the lot into the motel parking lot. In a short time, the motel would be full of paying customers. People passing the motel figured that if the motel parking lot was empty, the motel must not be very good. However, if the motel's parking lot was full, the passersby figured it must be a good place to stay. We follow others. And you have now become a person who is leading the world toward peace, understanding, and abundance for all.

A while back, I was awakened around 3 A.M. by coyotes howling in our pasture. The howling began with one lone coyote pup and spread among the pack. In a very short time, our two dogs picked up the howling. Soon our neighbors' dogs began to howl, and the howling crept up the valley in every direction as dogs on all sides joined in. After a while, I could hear dogs for miles in every direction howling. The coyotes had created a ripple and it was spreading. And it all began with just one small coyote pup.

> "One dog barks at something, the rest bark at him."
>
> —CHINESE PROVERB

Who you are creates an impact on your world. In the past

your impact may have been negative because of your propensity to complain. Now, however, you are modeling optimism and a better world for all. You are a ripple in the great ocean of humanity that resounds around the world.

You are a blessing.

COMPLAINT FREE WEDNESDAY

The opposite of complaining is gratitude. Gratitude is giving thanks for what you have, whereas complaining is expressing dissatisfaction with what you do not have. Before you can truly know gratitude, you must first stop complaining.

Just as the "Great American Smokeout" has been successful in getting smokers to go one day without smoking and thereby has raised public awareness as to the dangers of cigarettes, inspiring many to quit, so establishing Complaint Free Wednesday as the day before Thanksgiving will help people become mindful of how often they complain—and this is the first step toward becoming Complaint Free.

Take the lead in getting Complaint Free Wednesday designated in your town or city. The process is actually very simple. Many people have accomplished this where they live and raised awareness of the preponderance of complaining and its damaging effects.

STEP 1 Contact your mayor's office or city council. Tell them you are a local citizen and are part of A Complaint Free World, a worldwide program that has been embraced by more than ten million people in more than one hundred countries. Tell them it has been featured on *Oprah*, the *Today* show, and media around the world. Say that you want them to designate the day before Thanksgiving Complaint Free Wednesday.

STEP 2 Offer to send in the suggested proclamation found in Appendix B of this book. Ask when you can follow up and call or e-mail back to make certain it was received. Lastly, ask when it will be presented to the city council for a vote and tell them you will be present and that you will invite the media there to cover the event. Unless held in executive session, city council meetings are open to the public.

STEP 3 Send the press release also found in Appendix B to your local newspaper and TV and radio stations. Simply call the media outlets and ask, "To what e-mail address should I send a press release?" E-mail the press release, and call to make certain it is received. Then as the time for the council meeting approaches, call or e-mail the media to remind them.

Before I first tried this, I was nervous, until I discovered that city councils and mayor's offices make such designations all the time. They are typically eager to help, and they are often intrigued by this particular idea because they tend to deal with complaints all the time!

If I can help, e-mail me at Will@AComplaintFreeWorld .org. I would be happy to be interviewed or offer you support in any way.

Thank you for helping to spread this to others and to make our world Complaint Free.

SAMPLE PROCLAMATION AND PRESS RELEASE

Sample Proclamation

CONCURRENT RESOLUTION

Supporting the goals and ideals of Complaint Free Wednesday.

WHEREAS . . . The average person complains approximately 15 to 30 times per day, resulting in roughly 4.5 BILLION complaints spoken every day in the United States;

WHEREAS . . . Complaining keeps people focused on current problems, stultifying their innate abilities to seek and create positive, harmonious solutions;

WHEREAS . . . Complaining has been shown by research psychologists to be detrimental to a person's physical and emotional health, relationships, and to limit their career success;

WHEREAS . . . A Complaint Free World is a nonprofit organization that encourages people to stop complaining and redirect their minds toward more positive, constructive, and rewarding lives;

WHEREAS . . . A Complaint Free World has sent out more than 10 million Complaint Free purple bracelets to participants in 106 countries around the world who use them to monitor their success at achieving 21 consecutive Complaint Free days, thereby transforming their negative attitudes to positive;

WHEREAS . . . A Complaint Free World's intention is to transform the attitude of the world's people from negative to positive by inspiring no less than 1 percent of the global population (60 million people) to become Complaint Free;

WHEREAS . . . Thousands of schools in the United States have taken on the Complaint Free program, with tens of thousands of students of all ages achieving amazing results in creating positive attitudes;

THEREFORE, BE IT RESOLVED . . . The Mayor and City Council declare *COMPLAINT FREE WEDNESDAY* will be observed on the day before Thanksgiving this year and henceforth, providing each person in [Your Town or City] one day free from complaining in order to prepare for our national day of gratitude.

Sample Press Release

For Immediate Release

Contact: [Your Name]

Telephone: [Your Number]

E-mail: [Your E-mail Address]

Web: www.AComplaintFreeWorld.org

[Town/City] to proclaim the day before Thanksgiving
Complaint Free Wednesday

Mayor [Mayor's Name] and the city council of [Town/City] are joining other cities in the United States in designating the day before Thanksgiving Complaint Free Wednesday.

Complaining is the opposite of gratitude. Gratitude is giving thanks for what we have, whereas complaining is expressing dissatisfaction with what we do not have.

Before we can truly know gratitude, we must first stop complaining. This is the reason for establishing a day without complaint the day before our national day of gratitude.

Complaining keeps our focus on the problems at hand rather than looking for possible solutions.

Just as the "Great American Smokeout" has been successful in getting smokers to go one day without smoking and raised public awareness as to the dangers of cigarettes, thereby inspiring many to quit, establishing Complaint Free Wednesday as the day before Thanksgiving will help people become mindful of how often they complain, and this is the first step toward becoming Complaint Free.

How much more could [Town/City] achieve if, rather than focusing on our problems, we came together to look for solutions? This is the idea behind a Complaint Free World, which is an international phenomenon that has been featured on *Oprah*, the *Today* show, *The ABC Evening News*, and Fox News, and in *Newsweek*, the *Wall Street Journal*, *Chicken Soup for the Soul*, and more.

For more information on this proclamation, call [Your Name] at [Your Phone Number].

For more information on A Complaint Free World, visit www.A ComplaintFreeWorld.org, call Will Bowen at (816) 258-1288, or e-mail Will@AComplaintFreeWorld.org.

ACKNOWLEDGMENTS

Thank you first and foremost to Tom Alyea, who for the last five years has worked tirelessly and without remuneration to spread A Complaint Free World. Thank you to Dr. Maya Angelou for her inspiration and wisdom. Thank you to John Gladman, who has donated both his time and his considerable photographic and design talents to make us shine. Thank you to Anita Wixon, a true friend and ongoing Complaint Free cheerleader. Thank you to Sharon Winningham and Greg and Donna Baer for their love and support. Thank you to Robin Kowalski, whose research has helped me contextualize Complaint Free living. Thank you to Steve Hanselman of Level 5 Media, my literary agent and friend. Thank you to Crown Publishing/Doubleday for their continued support. Thank you to Marti Lee for modeling what is taught herein. Thank you to the countless volunteers who have packed and shipped millions upon millions of Complaint Free bracelets. Thank you to those who made financial donations small and large funding our work.

And thank you, dear reader, for being open to a new paradigm for your life and thereby helping to awaken our world.

CONNECT WITH US!

www.AComplaintFreeWorld.org

 facebook.com/AComplaintFreeWorld

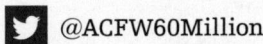 @ACFW60Million

**Visit our website and get your own
Complaint Free bracelet today!**